TALKING BACK

thinking feminist, thinking black

bell hooks

Between the Lines
Toronto

First published by South End Press
text design and production by Ellen Herman and South End Press
cover graphic by Charlotte Lewis; design by Loie Hayes

Grateful acknowledgement is made to the following publications fir permission to use previously published material: *Aurora, Catalyst, Discourse, Sage,* and *Zeta.*

This edition published by
Between the Lines
401 Richmond Street West
Studio 281
Toronto, Ontario M5V 3A8
Canada
1-800-718-7201
www.btlbooks.com

Every reasonable effort has been made to identify copyright holders. Between the Lines would be pleased to have any errors or omissions brought to its attention.

Cataloguing in Publication information available from Library and Archives Canada
ISBN 9780921284093

We acknowledge for their financial support of our publishing activities: the Government of Canada; the Canada Council for the Arts; and the Government of Ontario through the Ontario Arts Council, the Ontario Book Publishers Tax Credit program, and Ontario Creates.

Contents

1

introduction:
some opening remarks

This work came together in a slow way. Always something would get in the way—relationships ending, exile, loneliness, some recently discovered pain—and I had to hurt again, hurt myself all the way away from writing, re-writing, putting the book together. Finally I had to stop and check it out, as in "what's going on here." And there right in front of me, facing me, was the reason I was having so much trouble completing this work. In the other two books I had not said very much about myself— about Gloria Jean. There was a logic to this—a strategy, some thought behind my use of the pen name bell hooks and it was connected with feelings about representations of the self, about identity. And even when people would write stuff about me that had no relationship to me, things that were sometimes just not true, I had no urge to explain. But in this book I was doing things differently—and what was slowing me down had to do with disclosure, with what it means to reveal personal stuff. In the very construction of this book, *talking back,* laid out in the first essay, is the explanation for my uneasiness, my reluctance. It has to do with revealing the personal. It has to do with writing—with what it means to say things in print. It has to do with punishment—with all those years in childhood and on, where I was hurt for speaking truths, speaking the outrageous, speaking in my wild and witty way, or as friends sometimes say, "do we have to go that deep?"

Folks who know me in real life and in the unreal life of books can bear witness to a courageous openness in speech that often marks me, becomes that which I am known by. I am frank, direct, outspoken not just in talking about ideas but about that self—that me—which we are told is private, not public. Since *Feminist Theory: from margin to center* was published, I have had time to think even more critically about this split between public and private; time to experience and time to examine what I have experienced. In reflection, I see how deeply connected that split is to ongoing practices of domination (especially thinking about intimate relationships, ways racism, sexism, and class exploitation work in our daily lives, in those private spaces—that it is there that we are often most wounded, hurt, dehumanized; there that ourselves are most taken away, terrorized, and broken). The public reality and institutional structures of domination make the private space for oppression and exploitation concrete—real. That's why I think it crucial to talk about the points where the public and the private meet, to connect the two. And even folks who talk about ending domination seem to be afraid to break down the space separating the two.

In a private space with somebody I love—we were talking about honesty and openness. I had been talking about hard childhood experiences that we don't want to talk about and we were going on with each other about what should or should not be talked about. It came to me right then that there are some folks for whom openness is not about the luxury of "will I choose to share this or tell that," but rather, "will I survive—will I make it through—will I stay alive." And openness is about how to be well and telling the truth is about how to put the broken bits and pieces of the heart back together again. It is about being whole—being wholehearted.

The willingness to be open about personal stuff that has always been there for me in talking has only recently worked its way fully into my writing. It has taken longer for me to be publicly private in writing because there was lurking in me the fear of punishment—the fear of saying something about loved ones that they would feel should not be said. The fear that the punishment will be loss, that I will be cut off from meaningful contacts. This is truly, on a deep level, a real race and class issue 'cause so many black folks have been raised to believe that there is just so much that you should not talk about, not in private and not in public. So many poor and working-class people of all races have had the same stuff pushed down deep in them. One of the jokes we used to have about the "got everything" white people is how they just tell all their business, just put their stuff right out there. One point of blackness then became—like how you keep your stuff to yourself, how private you could be about your business. That's been a place where I've been hurt by family, by black folks outside family, by friends who say, "girl, you shouldn't even be talking about that!" And then it seemed all through graduate school, and when my first book was published, white folks were asking the same thing: "Do we want to hear what you are saying?" Seriously. It has been a political struggle for me to hold to the belief that there is much which we—black people—must speak about, much that is private that must be openly shared, if we are to heal our wounds (hurts caused by domination and exploitation and oppression), if we are to recover and realize ourselves.

When I gave talks, I spoke about my life much more than in my writing. Often it was that coming together of the idea, the theory, and shared personal experience that was the moment when the abstract became concrete, tangible, something people could hold and carry away with them. That was important to me. I learned with it. In all this talking, I was concerned that I not lose myself, my soul, that I not become an object, a spectacle. Part of being true to me was expressed in the effort to be genuine (not to be making myself into cheap entertainment), to be real (like what black folks mean when we say "get real"). There is this Native American Indian poem that has been with me in my heart for some time. It is a poem that speaks against betrayal, simple words: "we want what is real. We want what is real. Don't deceive us." The history of colonization, imperialism is a record of betrayal, of lies, and deceits. The demand for that which is real is a demand for reparation, for transformation. In resistance, the exploited, the oppressed work to expose the false reality—to reclaim and recover ourselves. We make the revolutionary history, telling the past as we have learned it mouth-to-mouth, telling the present as we see, know, and feel it in our hearts and with our words. In keeping with this spirit, I have approached these talks, essays, and comments by rooting them in personal reflection, in thinking feminist and thinking black.

Talking with students, with people who come to lectures, I have had the pain of fragmentation deeply impressed upon my consciousness. The alienation felt by many people who are concerned about domination—the struggle we have even to make of our words a language that can be shared, understood. There are times in this writing when it seems to me that I am saying what is already known, repeating myself, showing the respect I feel for Paulo Freire by quoting him much too often because he teaches me by his words, his presence. Yet it has been a humbling experience to talk about these feelings, the writing with other people, who remind me to accept that there may be much that I need to say for the sake of others that may not move or gratify me, that may not make people see me as "so smart." Or there may be much that I must say that I would rather keep silent—secret. Often I stopped myself from editing, from working to construct "the politically correct feminist thinker" with my words, so that I would just be there vulnerable, as I feel I am at times.

Then there are times when so much talk or writing, so many ideas seem to stand in the way, to block the awareness that for the oppressed, the exploited, the dominated, domination is not just a subject for radical discourse, for books. It is about pain—the pain of hunger, the pain of over-work, the pain of degradation and dehumanization, the pain of loneliness, the pain of loss, the pain of isolation, the pain of exile—spiritual and physical. Even before the words, we remember the pain. As comrades in struggle writing about the effort to end racial domination in South Africa put it in the *Freedom Charter:* "Our struggle is also a struggle of memory against forgetting."

2

talking back

In the world of the southern black community I grew up in, "back talk" and "talking back" meant speaking as an equal to an authority figure. It meant daring to disagree and sometimes it just meant having an opinion. In the "old school," children were meant to be seen and not heard. My great-grandparents, grandparents, and parents were all from the old school. To make yourself heard if you were a child was to invite punishment, the back-hand lick, the slap across the face that would catch you unaware, or the feel of switches stinging your arms and legs.

To speak then when one was not spoken to was a courageous act—an act of risk and daring. And yet it was hard not to speak in warm rooms where heated discussions began at the crack of dawn, women's voices filling the air, giving orders, making threats, fussing. Black men may have excelled in the art of poetic preaching in the male-dominated church, but in the church of the home, where the everyday rules of how to live and how to act were established, it was black women who preached. There, black women spoke in a language so rich, so poetic, that it felt to me like being shut off from life, smothered to death if one were not allowed to participate.

It was in that world of woman talk (the men were often silent, often absent) that was born in me the craving to speak, to have a voice, and not just any voice but one that could be identified as belonging to me. To make my voice, I had to speak, to hear myself talk—and talk I did—darting in and out of grown folks' conversations and dialogues, answering questions that were not directed at me, endlessly asking questions, making speeches. Needless to say, the punishments for these acts of speech seemed endless. They were intended to silence me—the child—and more particularly the girl child. Had I been a boy, they might have encouraged me to speak believing that I might someday be called to preach. There was no "calling" for talking girls, no legitimized rewarded speech. The punishments I received for "talking back" were intended to suppress all possibility that I would create my own speech. That speech was to be suppressed so that the "right speech of womanhood" would emerge.

Within feminist circles, silence is often seen as the sexist "right speech of womanhood"—the sign of woman's submission to patriarchal authority. This emphasis on woman's silence may be an accurate remembering of what has taken place in the households of women from WASP backgrounds in the United States, but in black communities (and diverse ethnic communities), women have not been silent. Their voices can be heard. Certainly for black women, our struggle has not been to emerge from silence into speech but to change the nature and direction of our speech, to make a speech that compels listeners, one that is heard.

Our speech, "the right speech of womanhood," was often the soliloquy, the talking into thin air, the talking to ears that do not hear you—the talk that is simply not listened to. Unlike the black male preacher whose speech was to be heard, who was to be listened to, whose words were to be remembered, the voices of black women—giving orders, making threats, fussing—could be tuned out, could become a kind of background music, audible but not acknowledged as significant speech. Dialogue—the sharing of speech and recognition—took place not between mother and child or mother and male authority figure but among black women. I can remember watching fascinated as our mother talked with her mother, sisters, and women friends. The intimacy and intensity of their speech—the satisfaction they received from talking to one another, the pleasure, the joy. It was in this world of woman speech, loud talk, angry words, women with tongues quick and sharp, tender sweet tongues, touching our world with their words, that I made speech my birthright—and the right to voice, to authorship, a privilege I would not be denied. It was in that world and because of it that I came to dream of writing, to write.

Writing was a way to capture speech, to hold onto it, keep it close. And so I wrote down bits and pieces of conversations, confessing in cheap diaries that soon fell apart from too much handling, expressing the intensity of my sorrow, the anguish of speech—for I was always saying the wrong thing, asking the wrong questions. I could not confine my speech to the necessary corners and concerns of life. I hid these writings under my bed, in pillow stuffings, among faded underwear. When my sisters found and read them, they ridiculed and mocked me—poking fun. I felt violated, ashamed, as if the secret parts of my self had been exposed,

brought into the open, and hung like newly clean laundry, out in the air for everyone to see. The fear of exposure, the fear that one's deepest emotions and innermost thoughts will be dismissed as mere nonsense, felt by so many young girls keeping diaries, holding and hiding speech, seems to me now one of the barriers that women have always needed and still need to destroy so that we are no longer pushed into secrecy or silence.

Despite my feelings of violation, of exposure, I continued to speak and write, choosing my hiding places well, learning to destroy work when no safe place could be found. I was never taught absolute silence, I was taught that it was important to speak but to talk a talk that was in itself a silence. Taught to speak and yet beware of the betrayal of too much heard speech, I experienced intense confusion and deep anxiety in my efforts to speak and write. Reciting poems at Sunday afternoon church service might be rewarded. Writing a poem (when one's time could be "better" spent sweeping, ironing, learning to cook) was luxurious activity, indulged in at the expense of others. Questioning authority, raising issues that were not deemed appropriate subjects brought pain, punishments—like telling mama I wanted to die before her because I could not live without her—that was crazy talk, crazy speech, the kind that would lead you to end up in a mental institution. "Little girl," I would be told, "if you don't stop all this crazy talk and crazy acting you are going to end up right out there at Western State."

Madness, not just physical abuse, was the punishment for too much talk if you were female. Yet even as this fear of madness haunted me, hanging over my writing like a monstrous shadow, I could not stop the words, making thought, writing speech. For this terrible madness which I feared, which I was sure was the destiny of daring women born to intense speech (after all, the authorities emphasized this point daily), was not as threatening as imposed silence, as suppressed speech.

Safety and sanity were to be sacrificed if I was to experience defiant speech. Though I risked them both, deep-seated fears and anxieties characterized my childhood days. I would speak but I would not ride a bike, play hardball, or hold the gray kitten. Writing about the ways we are traumatized in our growing-up years, psychoanalyst Alice Miller makes the point in *For Your Own Good* that it is not clear why childhood wounds become for some folk an opportunity to grow, to move forward rather than backward in the process of self-realization. Certainly, when I reflect on the trials of my growing-up years, the many punishments, I can see now that in resistance I learned to be vigilant in the nourishment of my spirit, to be tough, to courageously protect that spirit from forces that would break it.

While punishing me, my parents often spoke about the necessity of breaking my spirit. Now when I ponder the silences, the voices that are not heard, the voices of those wounded and/or oppressed individuals who do not speak or write, I contemplate the acts of persecution, torture—the terrorism that breaks spirits, that makes creativity impossible. I write these words to bear witness to the primacy of resistance struggle in any situation of domination (even within family life); to the strength and power that emerges from sustained resistance and the profound conviction that these forces can be healing, can protect us from dehumanization and despair.

These early trials, wherein I learned to stand my ground, to keep my spirit intact, came vividly to mind after I published *Ain't I A Woman* and the book was sharply and harshly criticized. While I had expected a climate of critical dialogue, I was not expecting a critical avalanche that had the power in its intensity to crush the spirit, to push one into silence. Since that time, I have heard stories about black women, about women of color, who write and publish (even when the work is quite successful) having nervous breakdowns, being made mad because they cannot bear the harsh responses of family, friends, and unknown critics, or becoming silent, unproductive. Surely, the absence of a humane critical response has tremendous impact on the writer from any oppressed, colonized group who endeavors to speak. For us, true speaking is not solely an expression of creative power; it is an act of resistance, a political gesture that challenges politics of domination that would render us nameless and voiceless. As such, it is a courageous act—as such, it represents a threat. To those who wield oppressive power, that which is threatening must necessarily be wiped out, annihilated, silenced.

Recently, efforts by black women writers to call attention to our work serve to highlight both our presence and absence. Whenever I peruse women's bookstores, I am struck not by the rapidly growing body of feminist writing by black women, but by the paucity of available published material. Those of us who write and are published remain few in number. The context of silence is varied and multi-dimensional. Most obvious are the ways racism, sexism, and class exploitation act to suppress and silence. Less obvious are the inner struggles, the efforts made to gain the necessary confidence to write, to re-write, to fully develop craft and skill—and the extent to which such efforts fail.

Although I have wanted writing to be my life-work since childhood, it has been difficult for me to claim "writer" as part of that which identifies and shapes my everyday reality. Even after publishing books, I would often speak of wanting to be a writer as though these works did not exist. And though I would be told, "you are a writer," I was not yet ready to fully affirm this truth. Part of myself was still held captive by domineering forces of history, of familial life that had charted a map of silence, of right speech. I had not completely let go of the fear of saying the wrong thing, of being punished. Somewhere in the deep recesses of my mind, I believed I could avoid both responsibility and punishment if I did not declare myself a writer.

One of the many reasons I chose to write using the pseudonym bell hooks, a family name (mother to Sarah Oldham, grandmother to Rosa Bell Oldham, great-grandmother to me), was to construct a writer-identity that would challenge and subdue all impulses leading me away from speech into silence. I was a young girl buying bubble gum at the corner store when I first really heard the full name bell hooks. I had just "talked back" to a grown person. Even now I can recall the surprised look, the mocking tones that informed me I must be kin to bell hooks—a sharp-tongued woman, a woman who spoke her mind, a woman who was not afraid to talk back. I claimed this legacy of defiance, of will, of courage, affirming my link to female ancestors who were bold and daring in their speech. Unlike my bold and daring mother and grandmother, who were not supportive of talking back, even though they were assertive and powerful in their speech, bell hooks as I discovered, claimed, and invented her was my ally, my support.

That initial act of talking back outside the home was empowering. It was the first of many acts of defiant speech that would make it possible for me to emerge as an independent thinker and writer. In retrospect, "talking back" became for me a rite of initiation, testing my courage, strengthening my commitment, preparing me for the days ahead—the days when writing, rejection notices, periods of silence, publication, ongoing development seem impossible but necessary.

Moving from silence into speech is for the oppressed, the colonized, the exploited, and those who stand and struggle side by side a gesture of defiance that heals, that makes new life and new growth possible. It is that act of speech, of "talking back," that is no mere gesture of empty words, that is the expression of our movement from object to subject—the liberated voice.

3

"when i was a young soldier for the revolution": coming to voice

Angela Davis spoke these words. They moved me. I say them here and hope to say them in many places. This is how deeply they touched me—evoking memories of innocence, of initial passionate commitment to political struggle. They were spoken in a talk she gave at a conference focussing on "Poetry and Politics: Afro-American Poetry Today." I began writing poetry when I was young, ten years old. Poetry came into my life, the sense of poetry, with reading scripture with those awkward and funny little rhymes we would memorize and recite on Easter Sunday. Then it came into my life at Booker T. Washington grade school where I learned that poetry was no silent subject. That moment of learning was pure enchantment, for we learned by listening and reciting that words put together just so, said just so, could have the same impact on our psyches as song, could lift and exalt our spirits, enabling us to feel tremendous joy, or carrying us down into that most immediate and violent sense of loss and grief.

Like many African-Americans, I became a writer through making poems. Poetry was one literary expression that was absolutely respected in our working-class household. Nights when the lights would go out, when storms were raging, we would sit in the dim candlelight of our living room and have a talent show. I would recite poems: Wordsworth, James Weldon Johnson, Langston Hughes, Elizabeth Barrett Browning, Emily Dick-

10

inson, Gwendolyn Brooks. poetry by white writers was always there in schools and on family bookshelves in anthologies of "great" works sold to us by door-to-door salesmen, book peddlers, who came spreading their wares as though we were a dark desert people and they weary travelers bringing us light from a faraway place. Poetry by black writers had to be searched for, a poem copied from books no one would let you borrow for fear of loss, or taken from books found by puzzled white southern librarians eager to see that you "read right." I was in high school before I discovered James Weldon Johnson's collection of *American Negro Poetry*. It had never been checked out of the library even though it had been on the shelves for some time. I would keep this book as long as I could, working to memorize every poem so I would know them all by heart.

For me, poetry was the place for the secret voice, for all that could not be directly stated or named, for all that would not be denied expression. Poetry was privileged speech—simple at times, but never ordinary. The magic of poetry was transformation; it was words changing shape, meaning, and form. Poetry was not mere recording of the way we southern black folks talked to one another, even though our language was poetic. It was transcendent speech. It was meant to transform consciousness, to carry the mind and heart to a new dimension. These were my primitive thoughts on poetry as I experienced and knew it growing up.

When I became a student in college creative writing classes, I learned a notion of "voice" as embodying the distinctive expression of an individual writer. Our efforts to become poets were to be realized in this coming into awareness and expression of one's voice. In all my writing classes, I was the only black student. Whenever I read a poem written in the particular dialect of southern black speech, the teacher and fellow students would praise me for using my "true," authentic voice, and encouraged me to develop this "voice," to write more of these poems. From the onset this troubled me. Such comments seemed to mask racial biases about what my authentic voice would or should be.

In part, attending all-black segregated schools with black teachers meant that I had come to understand black poets as being capable of speaking in many voices, that the Dunbar of a poem written in dialect was no more or less authentic than the Dunbar writing a sonnet. Yet it was listening to black musicians like Duke Ellington, Louis Armstrong, and later John Coltrane that impressed upon our consciousness a sense of versatility—they played all kinds of music, had multiple voices. So it was with poetry. The black poet, as exemplified by Gwendolyn Brooks and later Amiri Baraka, had many voices—with no single voice being identified as more or less authentic. The insistence on finding one voice, one definitive style of writing and reading one's poetry, fit all too neatly with a static notion of self and identity that was pervasive in university settings. It seemed that many black students found our situations problematic precisely because our sense of self, and by definition our voice, was not unilateral, monologist, or static but rather multi-dimensional. We were as at home in dialect as we were in standard English. Individuals who speak languages other than English, who speak patois as well as standard English, find it a necessary aspect of self-affirmation not to feel compelled to choose one voice over another, not to claim one as more authentic, but rather to construct social realities that celebrate, acknowledge, and affirm differences, variety. In *Borderlands: La Frontera*, Gloria Anzaldúa writes of the need to claim all the tongues in which we speak, to make speech of the many languages that give expression to the unique cultural reality of a people:

> For a people who are neither Spanish nor live in a country in which Spanish is the first language; for a people who live in a country in which English is the reigning tongue but who are not Anglo, for a people who cannot entirely identify with either standard (formal, Castilian) Spanish nor standard English, what recourse is left to them but to create their own language? A language which they can connect their identity to, one capable of communicating the realities and values true to themselves...

In recent years, any writing about feminism has overshadowed writing as a poet. Yet there are spaces where thoughts and concerns converge. One such space has been the feminist focus on coming to voice—on moving from silence into speech as revolutionary gesture. Once again, the idea of finding one's voice or having a voice assumes a primacy in talk, discourse, writing, and action. As metaphor for self-transformation, it has been especially relevant for groups of women who have previously never had a public voice, women who are speaking and writing for the first time, including many women of color. Feminist focus on finding a voice may seem clichéd at times, especially when the insistence is that women share a common speech or that all women have something meaningful to say at all times. However, for women within oppressed groups who have contained so many feelings—despair, rage, anguish—who do not speak, as poet Audre Lorde writes, "for fear our words will not be heard nor welcomed," coming to voice is an act of resistance. Speaking becomes both a way to engage in active self-transformation and a rite of passage where one moves from being object to being subject. Only as subjects can we speak. As objects, we remain voiceless—our beings defined and interpreted by others. It is this liberating speech that Mariana Romo-Carmona writes about in her introduction to *Compañeras: Latina Lesbians:*

> Each time a woman begins to speak, a liberating process begins, one that is unavoidable and has powerful political implications. In these pages we see repeated the process of self-discovery, of affirmation in coming out of the closet, the search for a definition of our identity within the family and out community, the search for answers, for mean-

ing in our personal struggles, and the commitment to a political struggle to end all forms of oppression. The stages of increasing awareness become clear when we begin to recount the story of our lives to someone else, someone who has experienced the same changes. When we write or speak about these changes we establish our experiences as valid and real, we begin to analyze, and that analysis gives us the necessary perspective to place our lives in a context where we know what to do next.

Awareness of the need to speak, to give voice to the varied dimensions of our lives, is one way women of color begin the process of education for critical consciousness.

Need for such speech is often validated in writings by people engaged in liberation struggles in the Third World, in the literatures of people struggling globally from oppression and domination. El Salvadoran writer Manlio Argueta structures his powerful novel, *One Day Of Life*, around the insistence on the development of political awareness, the sharing of knowledge that makes the revolutionary thinker and activist. It is the character José who is most committed to sharing his awareness with family and community, and most importantly with Lupé, his friend and wife, to whom he says:

> that's why the problems can't be solved by a single person, but only by all of us working together, the humble, the clearheaded ones. And this is very important; you can be humble and live in darkness. Well, the thing is not a matter of being or not being humble. The problem lies in our awareness. The awareness we will have. Then life will become as clear as spring water.

I first read this novel in a course I taught on Third World literature and it was clear then that speaking freely, openly has different meaning for people from exploited and oppressed groups.

Non-literary works by writers opposing domination also speak to the primacy of coming to voice, of speaking for the oppressed. In keeping with this emphasis on speech, Alicia Partnoy proclaims, in her brave work, *The Little School: Tales of Disappearance and Survival in Argentina*, "They cut off my voice so I grew two voices, into different tongues my songs I pour." Here speech has a dual implication. There is the silence of the oppressed who have never learned to speak and there is the voice of those who have been forcefully silenced because they have dared to speak and by doing so resist. Egyptian writer Nawal el Sa'adawi protests against such silences in her *Memoirs From The Women's Prison*. She dedicated her book "To all who have hated oppression to the point of death, who have loved freedom to the point of imprisonment, and have rejected falsehood to the point of revolution." Or the resistance to being silenced Theresa Had Cha describes in *Dictee:*

Mother, you are a child still. At eighteen. More of a child since you
are always ill. They have sheltered you from the others. It is not your
own. Even if it not you know you must. You are bi-lingual. You are
tri-lingual. The tongue that is forbidden is your own mother tongue.
You speak in the dark, in the secret. The one that is yours. Your
own...Mother tongue is your refuge. It is being home. Being who you
are. Truly. To speak makes you sad. To utter each word is a privilege
you risk by death.

In fiction as well as in confessional writing, those who understand the
power of voice as gesture of rebellion and resistance urge the exploited,
the oppressed to speak.

To speak as an act of resistance is quite different than ordinary talk,
or the personal confession that has no relation to coming into political
awareness, to developing critical consciousness. This is a difference we
must talk about in the United States, for here the idea of finding a voice
risks being trivialized or romanticized in the rhetoric of those who advocate a shallow feminist politic which privileges acts of speaking over the
content of speech. Such rhetoric often turns the voices and beings of non-
white women into commodity, spectacle. In a white-supremacist, capitalist,
patriarchal state where the mechanisms of co-optation are so advanced,
much that is potentially radical is undermined, turned into commodity,
fashionable speech as in "black women writers are in right now." Often
the question of who is listening and what is being heard are not answered.
When reggae music became popular in the Untied States, I often pondered
whether the privileged white people who listened were learning from this
music to resist, to rebel against white supremacy and white imperialism.
What did they hear when Bob Marley said, "we refuse to be what you
wanted us to be"—did they think about colonization, about internalized
racism? One night at a Jimmy Cliff concert attended predominantly by
young white people, Cliff began a call and response refrain where we the
listeners were to say "Africa for Africans." There was suddenly a hush in
the room, as though the listeners finally heard the rebellion against white
supremacy, against imperialism in the lyrics. They were silent, unable apparently to share in this gesture affirming black solidarity. Who is listening
and what do they hear?

Appropriation of the marginal voice threatens the very core of self-
determination and free self-expression for exploited and oppressed
peoples. If the identified audience, those spoken to, is determined solely
by ruling groups who control production and distribution, then it is easy
for the marginal voice striving for a hearing to allow what is said to be
overdetermined by the needs of that majority group who appears to be listening, to be tuned in. It becomes easy to speak about what that group
wants to hear, to describe and define experience in a language compatible
with existing images and ways of knowing, constructed within social

frameworks that reinforce domination. Within any situation of colonization, of domination, the oppressed, the exploited develop various styles of
relating, talking one way to one another, talking another way to those who
have power to oppress and dominate, talking in a way that allows one to
be understood by someone who does not know your way of speaking,
your language. The struggle to end domination, the individual struggle to
resist colonization, to move from object to subject, is expressed in the effort to establish the liberatory voice—that way of speaking that is no longer
determined by one's status as object—as oppressed being. That way of
speaking is characterized by opposition, by resistance. It demands that
paradigms shift—that we learn to talk—to listen—to hear in a new way.

To make the liberated voice, one must confront the issue of
audience—we must know to whom we speak. When I began writing my
first book, *Ain't I A Woman: black women and feminism*, the initial completed manuscript was excessively long and very repetitious. Reading it
critically, I saw that I was trying not only to address each different potential audience—black men, white women, white men, etc.—but that my
words were written to explain, to placate, to appease. They contained the
fear of speaking that often characterizes the way those in a lower position
within a hierarchy address those in a higher position of authority. Those
passages where I was speaking most directly to black women contained
the voice I felt to be most truly mine—it was then that my voice was daring,
courageous. When I thought about audience—the way in which the language we choose to use declares who it is we place at the center of our
discourse—I confronted my fear of placing myself and other black women
at the speaking center. Writing this book was for me a radical gesture. It
not only brought me face-to-face with this question of power; it forced me
to resolve this question, to act, to find my voice, to become that subject
who could place herself and those like her at the center of feminist discourse. I was transformed in consciousness and being.

When the book was first published, white women readers would
often say to me, "I don't feel this book is really talking to me." Often these
readers would interpret the direct, blunt speech as signifying anger and I
would have to speak against this interpretation and insist upon the difference between direct speech and hostility. At a discussion once where a
question about audience was raised, I responded by saying that while I
would like readers to be diverse, the audience I most wanted to address
was black women, that I wanted to place us at the center. I was asked by
a white woman, "How can you do that in a cultural context where black
women are not primary book buyers and white women are the principle
buyers of feminist books?" It seemed that she was suggesting that audience
should be determined by who buys certain books. It had never occurred
to me that white women would not buy a book if they did not see themselves at the center because, more than any group of people I could iden-

tify, white people have travelled the globe consuming cultural artifacts that did not place them at the center. My placement of black women at the center was not an action to exclude others but rather an invitation, a challenge to those who would hear us speak, to shift paradigms rather than appropriate, to have all readers listen to the voice of a black woman speaking a subject and not as underprivileged other. I wrote *Ain't I A Woman* not to inform white women about black women but rather as an expression of my longing to know more and think deeply about our experience.

In celebrating our coming to voice, Third World women, African-American women must work against speaking as "other," speaking to difference as it is constructed in the white-supremacist imagination. It is therefore crucial that we search our hearts and our words to see if our true aim is liberation, to make sure they do not suppress, trap, or confine. Significantly, knowing who is listening provides an indication of how our voices are heard. My words are heard differently by the oppressive powerful. They are heard in a different way by black women who, like me, are struggling to recover ourselves from the ravages of colonization. To know our audience, to know who listens, we must be in dialogue. We must be speaking with and not just speaking to. In hearing responses, we come to understand whether our words act to resist, to transform, to move. In a consumer culture where we are all led to believe that the value of our voice is not determined by the extent to which it challenges, or makes critical reflection possible, but rather by whether or not it (and sometimes even we) is liked, it is difficult to keep a liberatory message. It is difficult to maintain a sense of direction, a strategy for liberated speaking, if we do not constantly challenge these standards of valuation. When I first began to talk publicly about my work, I would be disappointed when audiences were provoked and challenged but seemed to disapprove. Not only was my desire for approval naive (I have since come to understand that it is silly to think that one can challenge and also have approval), it was dangerous precisely because such a longing can undermine radical commitment, compelling a change in voice so as to gain regard.

Speaking out is not a simple gesture of freedom in a culture of domination. We are often deceived (yes, even those of us who have experienced domination) by the illusion of free speech, falsely believing that we can say whatever we wish in an atmosphere of openness. There would be no need to even speak of the oppressed and exploited coming to voice, articulating and redefining reality, if there were not oppressive mechanisms of silencing, suppressing, and censoring. Thinking we speak in a climate where freedom is valued, we are often shocked to find ourselves assaulted, our words devalued. It should be understood that the liberatory voice will necessarily confront, disturb, demand that listeners even alter ways of hearing and being. I remember talking with Angela Davis a few years ago about the death threats that she often received before speaking. Our conversation had a profound effect on my consciousness, on me as a listener; it changed my understanding of what it means to speak from a radical position in this society. When one threatens—one is at risk.

Often I am amazed as a teacher in the classroom at the extent to which students are afraid to speak. A young black woman student wrote these words to me:

> My voice is not fit to be heard by 120 people. To produce such a voice, my temperature increases and my hands shake. My voice is calm and quiet and soothing; it is not a means of announcing the many secrets my friends have told me—it quiets the rush of the running stream that is their life, slowing to make a mirror to reflect their worries, so that they can be examined and problems rectified. I am not relieved by voicing my opinions. Placing my opinion up to be judged by the public is a form of opening myself to criticism and pain. Those who do not share my eyes cannot see where to tread lightly on me.
>
> I am afraid. I am, and will always be afraid. My fear is that I will not be understood. I try to learn the vocabulary of my friends to ensure my communication on their terms. There is no singular vocabulary of 120 people. I will be misunderstood; I will not be respected as a speaker; they will name me Stupid in their minds; they will disregard me. I am afraid.

Encouraging students to speak, I tell them to imagine what it must mean to live in a culture where to speak one risks brutal punishment—imprisonment, torture, death. I ask them to think about what it means that they lack the courage to speak in a culture where there are few if any consequences. Can their fear be understood solely as shyness or is it an expression of deeply embedded, socially constructed restrictions against speech in a culture of domination, a fear of owning one's words, of taking a stand? Audre Lorde's poem, "Litany for Survival," addresses our fear of speech and urges us to overcome it:

> and when we speak we are afraid
> our words will not be heard
> nor welcomed
> but when we are silent
> we are still afraid
>
> So it is better to speak
> remembering
> we were never meant to survive.

To understand that finding a voice is an essential part of liberation struggle—for the oppressed, the exploited a necessary starting place—a move in the direction of freedom, is important for those who stand in solidarity with us. That talk which identifies us as uncommitted, as lacking in critical consciousness, which signifies a condition of oppression and exploitation, is utterly transformed as we engage in critical reflection and as we act to resist domination. We are prepared to struggle for freedom only when this groundwork has been laid.

When we dare to speak in a liberatory voice, we threaten even those who may initially claim to want our words. In the act of overcoming our fear of speech, of being seen as threatening, in the process of learning to speak as subjects, we participate in the global struggle to end domination. When we end our silence, when we speak in a liberated voice, our words connect us with anyone, anywhere who lives in silence. Feminist focus on women finding a voice, on the silence of black women, of women of color, has led to increased interest in our words. This is an important historical moment. We are both speaking of our own volition, out of our commitment to justice, to revolutionary struggle to end domination, and simultaneously called to speak, "invited" to share our words. It is important that we speak. What we speak about is more important. It is our responsibility collectively and individually to distinguish between mere speaking that is about self-aggrandizement, exploitation of the exotic "other," and that coming to voice which is a gesture of resistance, an affirmation of struggle.

4

feminism: a transformational politic

We live in a world in crisis—a world governed by politics of domination, one in which the belief in a notion of superior and inferior, and its concomitant ideology—that the superior should rule over the inferior—effects the lives of all people everywhere, whether poor or privileged, literate or illiterate. Systematic dehumanization, worldwide famine, ecological devastation, industrial contamination, and the possibility of nuclear destruction are realities which remind us daily that we are in crisis. Contemporary feminist thinkers often cite sexual politics as the origin of this crisis. They point to the insistence on difference as that factor which becomes the occasion for separation and domination and suggest that differentiation of status between females and males globally is an indication that patriarchal domination of the planet is the root of the problem. Such an assumption has fostered the notion that elimination of sexist oppression would necessarily lead to the eradication of all forms of domination. It is an argument that has led influential Western white women to feel that feminist movement should be *the* central political agenda for females globally. Ideologically, thinking in this direction enables Western women, especially privileged white women, to suggest that racism and class exploitation are merely the offspring of the parent system: patriarchy. Within feminist movement in the West, this has led to the assumption that resisting patriarchal domination is a more legitimate feminist action than resisting racism and other forms of domination. Such thinking prevails despite radical critiques

19

made by black women and other women of color who question this proposition. To speculate that an oppositional division between men and women existed in early human communities is to impose on the past, on these non-white groups, a world view that fits all too neatly within contemporary feminist paradigms that name man as the enemy and woman as the victim.

Clearly, differentiation between strong and weak, powerful and powerless, has been a central defining aspect of gender globally, carrying with it the assumption that men should have greater authority than women, and should rule over them. As significant and important as this fact is, it should not obscure the reality that women can and do participate in politics of domination, as perpetrators as well as victims—that we dominate, that we are dominated. If focus on patriarchal domination masks this reality or becomes the means by which women deflect attention from the real conditions and circumstances of our lives, then women cooperate in suppressing and promoting false consciousness, inhibiting our capacity to assume responsibility for transforming ourselves and society.

Thinking speculatively about early human social arrangement, about women and men struggling to survive in small communities, it is likely that the parent-child relationship with its very real imposed survival structure of dependency, of strong and weak, of powerful and powerless, was a site for the construction of a paradigm of domination. While this circumstance of dependency is not necessarily one that leads to domination, it lends itself to the enactment of a social drama wherein domination could easily occur as a means of exercising and maintaining control. This speculation does not place women outside the practice of domination, in the exclusive role of victim. It centrally names women as agents of domination, as potential theoreticians, and creators of a paradigm for social relationships wherein those groups of individuals designated as "strong" exercise power both benevolently and coercively over those designated as "weak."

Emphasizing paradigms of domination that call attention to woman's capacity to dominate is one way to deconstruct and challenge the simplistic notion that man is the enemy, woman the victim; the notion that men have always been the oppressors. Such thinking enables us to examine our role as women in the perpetuation and maintenance of systems of domination. To understand domination, we must understand that our capacity as women and men to be either dominated or dominating is a point of connection, of commonality. Even though I speak from the particular experience of living as a black woman in the United States, a white-supremacist, capitalist, patriarchal society, where small numbers of white men (and honorary "white men") constitute ruling groups, I understand that in many places in the world oppressed and oppressor share the same color. I understand that right here in this room, oppressed and oppressor share the same gender. Right now as I speak, a man who is himself victimized, wounded, hurt by racism and class exploitation is actively dominating a woman in his life—that even as I speak, women who are ourselves exploited, victimized, are dominating children. It is necessary for us to remember, as we think critically about domination, that we all have the capacity to act in ways that oppress, dominate, wound (whether or not that power is institutionalized). It is necessary to remember that it is first the potential oppressor within that we must resist—the potential victim within that we must rescue—otherwise we cannot hope for an end to domination, for liberation.

This knowledge seems especially important at this historical moment when black women and other women of color have worked to create awareness of the ways in which racism empowers white women to act as exploiters and oppressors. Increasingly this fact is considered a reason we should not support feminist struggle even though sexism and sexist oppression is a real issue in our lives as black women (see, for example, Vivian Gordon's *Black Women, Feminism, Black Liberation: Which Way?*). It becomes necessary for us to speak continually about the convictions that inform our continued advocacy of feminist struggle. By calling attention to interlocking systems of domination—sex, race, and class—black women and many other groups of women acknowledge the diversity and complexity of female experience, of our relationship to power and domination. The intent is not to dissuade people of color from becoming engaged in feminist movement. Feminist struggle to end patriarchal domination should be of primary importance to women and men globally not because it is the foundation of all other oppressive structures but because it is that form of domination we are most likely to encounter in an ongoing way in everyday life.

Unlike other forms of domination, sexism directly shapes and determines relations of power in our private lives, in familiar social spaces, in that most intimate context—home—and in that most intimate sphere of relations—family. Usually, it is within the family that we witness coercive domination and learn to accept it, whether it be domination of parent over child, or male over female. Even though family relations may be, and most often are, informed by acceptance of a politic of domination, they are simultaneously relations of care and connection. It is this convergence of two contradictory impulses—the urge to promote growth and the urge to inhibit growth—that provides a practical setting for feminist critique, resistance, and transformation.

Growing up in a black, working-class, father-dominated household, I experienced coercive adult male authority as more immediately threatening, as more likely to cause immediate pain than racist oppression or class exploitation. It was equally clear that experiencing exploitation and oppression in the home made one feel all the more powerless when encountering dominating forces outside the home. This is true for many people. If we are unable to resist and end domination in relations where there is care, it seems totally unimaginable that we can resist and end it in other institutionalized relations of power. If we cannot convince the mothers and/or fathers who care not to humiliate and degrade us, how can we imagine convincing or resisting an employer, a lover, a stranger who systematically humiliates and degrades?

Feminist effort to end patriarchal domination should be of primary concern precisely because it insists on the eradication of exploitation and oppression in the family context and in all other intimate relationships. It is that political movement which most radically addresses the person—the personal—citing the need for transformation of self, of relationships, so that we might be better able to act in a revolutionary manner, challenging and resisting domination, transforming the world outside the self. Strategically, feminist movement should be a central component of all other liberation struggles because it challenges each of us to alter our person, our personal engagement (either as victims or perpetrators or both) in a system of domination.

Feminism, as liberation struggle, must exist apart from and as a part of the larger struggle to eradicate domination in all its forms. We must understand that patriarchal domination shares an ideological foundation with racism and other forms of group oppression, that there is no hope that it can be eradicated while these systems remain intact. This knowledge should consistently inform the direction of feminist theory and practice. Unfortunately, racism and class elitism among women has frequently led to the suppression and distortion of this connection so that it is now necessary for feminist thinkers to critique and revise much feminist theory and the direction of feminist movement. This effort at revision is perhaps most evident in the current widespread acknowledgement that sexism, racism, and class exploitation constitute interlocking systems of domination—that sex, race, and class, and not sex alone, determine the nature of any female's identity, status, and circumstance, the degree to which she will or will not be dominated, the extent to which she will have the power to dominate.

While acknowledgement of the complex nature of woman's status (which has been most impressed upon everyone's consciousness by radical women of color) is a significant corrective, it is only a starting point. It provides a frame of reference which must serve as the basis for thoroughly altering and revising feminist theory and practice. It challenges and calls us to re-think popular assumptions about the nature of feminism that have had the deepest impact on a large majority of women, on mass consciousness. It radically calls into question the notion of a fundamentally common female experience which has been seen as the prerequisite for our coming together, for political unity. Recognition of the inter-connectedness of sex, race, and class highlights the diversity of experience, compelling redefinition of the terms for unity. If women do not share "common oppression," what then can serve as a basis for our coming together?

Unlike many feminist comrades, I believe women and men must share a common understanding—a basic knowledge of what feminism is—if it is ever to be a powerful mass-based political movement. In *Feminist Theory: from margin to center,* I suggest that defining feminism broadly as "a movement to end sexism and sexist oppression" would enable us to have a common political goal. We would then have a basis on which to build solidarity. Multiple and contradictory definitions of feminism create confusion and undermine the effort to construct feminist movement so that it addresses everyone. Sharing a common goal does not imply that women and men will not have radically divergent perspectives on how that goal might be reached. Because each individual starts the process of engagement in feminist struggle at a unique level of awareness, very real differences in experience, perspective, and knowledge make developing varied strategies for participation and transformation a necessary agenda.

Feminist thinkers engaged in radically revisioning central tenets of feminist thought must continually emphasize the importance of sex, race and class as factors which *together* determine the social construction of femaleness, as it has been so deeply ingrained in the consciousness of many women active in feminist movement that gender is the sole factor determining destiny. However, the work of education for critical consciousness (usually called consciousness-raising) cannot end there. Much feminist consciousness-raising has in the past focussed on identifying the particular ways men oppress and exploit women. Using the paradigm of sex, race, and class means that the focus does not begin with men and what they do to women, but rather with women working to identify both individually and collectively the specific character of our social identity.

Imagine a group of women from diverse backgrounds coming together to talk about feminism. First they concentrate on working out their status in terms of sex, race, and class using this as the standpoint from which they begin discussing patriarchy or their particular relations with individual men. Within the old frame of reference, a discussion might consist solely of talk about their experiences as victims in relationship to male oppressors. Two women—one poor, the other quite wealthy—might describe the process by which they have suffered physical abuse by male partners and find certain commonalities which might serve as a basis for bonding. Yet if these same two women engaged in a discussion of class, not only would the social construction and expression of femaleness differ, so too would their ideas about how to confront and change their circumstances. Broadening the discussion to include an analysis of race and class would expose many additional differences even as commonalities emerged.

Clearly the process of bonding would be more complex, yet this broader discussion might enable the sharing of perspectives and strategies for change that would enrich rather than diminish our understanding of gender. While feminists have increasingly given "lip service" to the idea of diversity, we have not developed strategies of communication and inclusion that allow for the successful enactment of this feminist vision.

Small groups are no longer the central place for feminist consciousness-raising. Much feminist education for critical consciousness takes place in Women's Studies classes or at conferences which focus on gender. Books are a primary source of education which means that already masses of people who do not read have no access. The separation of grassroots ways of sharing feminist thinking across kitchen tables from the spheres where much of that thinking is generated, the academy, undermines feminist movement. It would further feminist movement if new feminist thinking could be once again shared in small group contexts, integrating critical analysis with discussion of personal experience. It would be useful to promote anew the small group setting as an arena for education for critical consciousness, so that women and men might come together in neighborhoods and communities to discuss feminist concerns.

Small groups remain an important place for education for critical consciousness for several reasons. An especially important aspect of the small group setting is the emphasis on communicating feminist thinking, feminist theory, in a manner that can be easily understood. In small groups, individuals do not need to be equally literate or literate at all because the information is primarily shared through conversation, in dialogue which is necessarily a liberatory expression. (Literacy should be a goal for feminists even as we ensure that it not become a requirement for participation in feminist education.) Reforming small groups would subvert the appropriation of feminist thinking by a select group of academic women and men, usually white, usually from privileged class backgrounds.

Small groups of people coming together to engage in feminist discussion, in dialectical struggle make a space where the "personal is political" as a starting point for education for critical consciousness can be extended to include politicization of the self that focusses on creating understanding of the ways sex, race, and class together determine our individual lot and our collective experience. It would further feminist movement if many well known feminist thinkers would participate in small groups, critically re-examining ways their works might be changed by incorporating broader perspectives. All efforts at self-transformation challenge us to engage in ongoing, critical self-examination and reflection about feminist practice, about how we live in the world. This individual commitment, when coupled with engagement in collective discussion, provides a space for critical feedback which strengthens our efforts to change and make ourselves new. It is in this commitment to feminist principles in our words and deeds that the hope of feminist revolution lies.

Working collectively to confront difference, to expand our awareness of sex, race, and class as interlocking systems of domination, of the ways we reinforce and perpetuate these structures, is the context in which we learn the true meaning of solidarity. It is this work that must be the foundation of feminist movement. Without it, we cannot effectively resist patriarchal domination; without it, we remain estranged and alienated from one another. Fear of painful confrontation often leads women and men active in feminist movement to avoid rigorous critical encounter, yet if we cannot engage dialectically in a committed, rigorous, humanizing manner, we cannot hope to change the world. True politicization—coming to critical consciousness—is a difficult, "trying" process, one that demands that we give up set ways of thinking and being, that we shift our paradigms, that we open ourselves to the unknown, the unfamiliar. Undergoing this process, we learn what it means to struggle and in this effort we experience the dignity and integrity of being that comes with revolutionary change. If we do not change our consciousness, we cannot change our actions or demand change from others.

Our renewed commitment to a rigorous process of education for critical consciousness will determine the shape and direction of future feminist movement. Until new perspectives are created, we cannot be living symbols of the power of feminist thinking. Given the privileged lot of many leading feminist thinkers, both in terms of status, class, and race, it is harder these days to convince women of the primacy of this process of politicization. More and more, we seem to form select interest groups composed of individuals who share similar perspectives. This limits our capacity to engage in critical discussion. It is difficult to involve women in new processes of feminist politicization because so many of us think that identifying men as the enemy, resisting male domination, gaining equal access to power and privilege is the end of feminist movement. Not only is it not the end, it is not even the place we want revitalized feminist movement to begin. We want to begin as women seriously addressing ourselves, not solely in relation to men, but in relation to an entire structure of domination of which patriarchy is one part. While the struggle to eradicate sexism and sexist oppression is and should be the primary thrust of feminist movement, to prepare ourselves politically for this effort we must first learn how to be in solidarity, how to struggle with one another.

Only when we confront the realities of sex, race, and class, the ways they divide us, make us different, stand us in opposition, and work to reconcile and resolve these issues will we be able to participate in the making of feminist revolution, in the transformation of the world. Feminism, as Charlotte Bunch emphasizes again and again in *Passionate Politics,* is a transformational politics, a struggle against domination wherein the effort is to change ourselves as well as structures. Speaking about the struggle to confront difference, Bunch asserts:

> A crucial point of the process is understanding that reality does not look the same from different people's perspective. It is not surprising that one way feminists have come to understand about differences has been through the love of a person from another culture or race. It takes persistence and motivation—which love often engenders—to get beyond one's ethnocentric assumptions and really learn about other perspectives. In this process and while seeking to eliminate oppression, we also discover new possibilities and insights that come from the experience and survival of other peoples.

Embedded in the commitment to feminist revolution is the challenge to love. Love can be and is an important source of empowerment when we struggle to confront issues of sex, race, and class. Working together to identify and face our differences—to face the ways we dominate and are dominated—to change our actions, we need a mediating force that can sustain us so that we are not broken in this process, so that we do not despair.

Not enough feminist work has focussed on documenting and sharing ways individuals confront differences constructively and successfully. Women and men need to know what is on the other side of the pain experienced in politicization. We need detailed accounts of the ways our lives are fuller and richer as we change and grow politically, as we learn to live each moment as committed feminists, as comrades working to end domination. In reconceptualizing and reformulating strategies for future feminist movement, we need to concentrate on the politicization of love, not just in the context of talking about victimization in intimate relationships, but in a critical discussion where love can be understood as a powerful force that challenges and resists domination. As we work to be loving, to create a culture that celebrates life, that makes love possible, we move against dehumanization, against domination. In *Pedagogy of the Oppressed*, Paulo Freire evokes this power of love, declaring:

> I am more and more convinced that true revolutionaries must perceive the revolution, because of its creative and liberating nature, as an act of love. For me, the revolution, which is not possible without a theory of revolution—and therefore science—is not irreconcilable with love...The distortion imposed on the word "love" by the capitalist world cannot prevent the revolution from being essentially loving in character, nor can it prevent the revolutionaries from affirming their love of life.

That aspect of feminist revolution that calls women to love womanness, that calls men to resist dehumanizing concepts of masculinity, is an essential part of our struggle. It is the process by which we move from seeing ourselves as objects to acting as subjects. When women and men understand that working to eradicate patriarchal domination is a struggle rooted in the longing to make a world where everyone can live fully and freely, then we know our work to be a gesture of love. Let us draw upon that love to heighten our awareness, deepen our compassion, intensify our courage, and strengthen our commitment.

5

on self-recovery

Often when the radical voice speaks about domination we are speaking to those who dominate. Their presence changes the direction and shape of our words. Language is also a place of struggle. I was just a girl coming slowly into womanhood when I read Adrienne Rich's words: "This is the oppressor's language, yet I need to talk to you." This language that enabled me to finish graduate school, to write a dissertation, to talk at job interviews, carries the scent of oppression. The Australian aborigines say: "The smell of the white man is killing us." I remember the smells of my childhood: hot water cornbread, turnip greens, fried pies. I remember the way we talked to one another, our words thickly accented black southern speech. We are rooted in language, wedded, have our being in words. Language is also a place of struggle. The oppressed struggle in language to recover ourselves—to rewrite, to reconcile, to renew. Our words are not without meaning. They are an action—a resistance. Language is also a place of struggle.

Dare I speak to oppressed and oppressor in the same voice? Dare I speak to you in a language that will take us away from the boundaries of domination, a language that will not fence you in, bind you, or hold you. Language is also a place of struggle. The oppressed struggle in language to read ourselves—to reunite, to reconcile, to renew. Our words are not without meaning. They are an action—a resistance. Language is also a place of struggle.

28

Lately, I struggle to be a woman of my word. Black woman poet Mari Evans urges us, "Speak truth to the people." The academic setting, the academic discourse I work in, is not a known site for truthtelling. It is not a place where the oppressed gather to talk our way out of bondage, to write our way into freedom, publishing articles and books that do more than inform, that testify, bearing witness to the primacy of struggle, to our collective effort to transform. Yet this is our most urgent need, the most important of our work—the work of liberation. Trapped as we often are in a cultural context that defines freedom solely in terms of learning the oppressor's language (language as culture; learning to live the oppressor's culture, what Baba, my grandmother, what Native American Indians before her called "learning the white man's ways"); assimilating however slowly into the dominant hegemony, into the mainstream. It has been extremely difficult to move beyond this shallow, empty version of what we can do, mere imitators of our oppressors, toward a liberatory vision—one that transforms our consciousness, our very being.

The most important of our work—the work of liberation—demands of us that we make a new language, that we create the oppositional discourse, the liberatory voice. Fundamentally, the oppressed person who has moved from object to subject speaks to us in a new way. This speech, this liberatory voice, emerges only when the oppressed experience self-recovery. Paolo Freire asserts in *Pedagogy of the Oppressed*, "We cannot enter the struggle as objects in order to later become subjects." The act of becoming subject is yet another way to speak the process of self-recovery.

Reflecting on the Vietnam War in the early 1970s—on protests and resistance—Buddhist monk Thich Nhat Hanhn spoke in conversation with Daniel Berrigan about the way forces of domination fragment, estrange, and assault our innermost beings, breaking us apart. He spoke about the need to restore the self to a condition of wholeness: "In French they have the word *recueillement* to describe the attitude of someone trying to be himself or herself, not to be dispersed, one member of the body here, another there. One tries to recover, to be once more in good shape, to become whole again." His words were especially moving to me, as I came to them at a time in life when I had not fully developed critical consciousness, when I was lost yet still seeking, trying to understand myself and the world around me. These words lingered in my consciousness:

In the Buddhist tradition, people used to speak of 'enlightenment' as a kind of returning home. The three worlds—the worlds of form, of non-form, of desire—are not your homes. These are places where you wander around for many existences, alienated from your own nature. So enlightenment is the way to get back. And they speak about efforts to go back—described in terms of the recovery of oneself, of one's integrity.

Nhat Hanhn's words placed in my consciousness the idea of self-recovery. Though speaking to a political issue, anti-war protest, he talks about self-recovery in spiritual terms (which also has deep meaning for me). In my thinking, I linked self-recovery again and again with the over-all effort of the oppressed, the dominated, to develop awareness of those forces which exploit and oppress; with efforts to educate for critical consciousness, to create effective and meaningful resistance, to make revolutionary transformation. Toni Cade Bambara, editor of the anthology *The Black Woman*, in her groundbreaking essay, "On the Issue of Roles," emphasizes "revolution begins with the self and in the self." Heeding her words, I became all the more vigilant in my effort to practice sustained, rigorous, critical self-examination. As I moved beyond the boundaries of our small, segregated southern black community into the university, into the larger world, I realized (and it was a painful and potentially devastating realization) that I did not understand fully what it meant to be a black woman in the United States, the politics of our reality. I began to search desperately for the understanding. That search ultimately led me to Women's Studies classes, to feminist writing, places where I then did not find what I needed to nourish my spirit. It was then that I began writing *Ain't I a Woman: Black Women and Feminism,* although it was not published until years later, when a space was created within feminist movement in the United States wherein the voices of black women could be acknowledged and heard.

Now I say, "*Ain't I a Woman* is the book of my self-recovery, the expression of my awakening to critical consciousness." I say, "It is the book of my heart, that I will not write such a book again." I say this now. Then it was experienced, and felt, as a private joy—then I had no language to speak this joy in political terms. Writing this book, I was compelled to confront black women's reality, our denied and buried history, our present circumstances. The thinking, the writing, was an act of reclamation, enabling me to recover myself, to be whole.

I call this experience "self-recovery." Still, I had to live with this term to think it through critically. I was particularly uncertain about the words "self-recovery," the insistence in them that a wholeness of being—named here the self—is present, possible, that we have experienced it, that it is a state to which we can return. I wanted to know in my heart if this was true for the oppressed, the dominated, the dehumanized, that the conditions for wholeness, that the whole self existed prior to exploitation and oppression, a self that could indeed be restored, recovered.

Discarding the notion that the self exists in opposition to an other that must be destroyed, annihilated (for when I left the segregated world of home and moved in and among white people, and their ways of knowing, I learned this way of understanding the social construction of self). I evoked the way of knowing I had learned from unschooled southern black folks. We learned that the self existed in relation, was dependent for its

very being on the lives and experiences of everyone, the self not as signifier of one "I" but the coming together of many "I"s, the self as embodying collective reality past and present, family and community. Social
construction of the self in relation would mean, then, that we would know
the voices that speak in and to us from the past, that we would be in touch
with what Paule Marshall calls "our ancient properties"—our history. Yet
it is precisely these voices that are silenced, suppressed, when we are
dominated. It is this collective voice we struggle to recover. Domination
and colonization attempt to destroy our capacity to know the self, to know
who we are. We oppose this violation, this dehumanization, when we seek
self-recovery, when we work to reunite fragments of being, to recover our
history. This process of self-recovery enables us to see ourselves as if for
the first time, for our field of vision is no longer shaped and determined
solely by the condition of domination. In Carol Stack's recent work on
black folks leaving the North to return South, Joella, the black woman who
speaks in a subject-to-subject way to a white woman for the first time, says
of this speaking, "It was like a voice came out of me that I did not know
was there. And I was hearing this voice for the first time. I was speaking
with my own voice." Years ago, I did not feel the need to tell the story of
my self-recovery, how this work, the research, its revelations, gave me a
sense of being, a grounding, because no framework existed in the United
States privileging this confrontation with reality. Now I understand that the
process by which the colonized, the oppressed, sever our ties, our complicity with the colonizer, the oppressor, constitutes a liberatory model for
social change, a strategy of resistance that must be shared, that must be
talked about.

Within radical political movements in the United States, this process
of self-recovery, of education for critical consciousness, remains in many
ways an unacknowledged process. Unlike revolutionary struggles globally, where it is deemed essential to the process of radicalization, models of
radical social change in the U.S. often de-emphasize focus on the ways individuals develop political consciousness. There are no literacy programs
here that also educate for critical consciousness. Concurrently, it is often
assumed that those who have the privilege of university education do not
need education for critical consciousness. This is a grave mistake. No radical change, no revolutionary transformation will occur in this society—in
this culture of domination—if we refuse to acknowledge the necessity for
radicalizing consciousness in conjunction with collective political resistance. When I speak about radicalizing consciousness, I think of the word
concientizacion, which implies much more than the mere adoption of
politically correct slogans or support for politically correct causes.

We must envision the university as a central site for revolutionary
struggle, a site where we can work to educate for critical consciousness,
where we can have a pedagogy of liberation. Yet how can we transform
others if our habits of being reinforce and perpetuate domination in all its

forms: racism, sexism, class exploitation? This returns us to the issue of self-recovery, extending it to include models of personal transformation that address both the oppressor and oppressed. In Nancy Hartsock's recent work on creating new epistomologies, she recalls the work of Albert Memmi and his insistence that both colonizer and colonized are dehumanized, albeit in different and very distinct ways within a culture of domination. Therefore, if domination is to end, there must be personal transformation on both sides. For those of us who oppose and resist domination, whether we be dominated or dominators, there is the shared longing for personal transformation, for the remaking and reconstituting of ourselves so that we can be radical.

It is crucial that we not ignore the self nor the longing people have to transform the self, that we make the conditions for wholeness such that they are mirrored both in our own beings and in social and political reality.

Using contemporary feminist movement as an example, we can look at ways feminist activists try to educate for critical consciousness. Within contemporary feminist movement, the process of consciousness-raising was at one time a central framework for the development of critical consciousness. Yet often the focus was solely one of naming one's oppressor, naming the pain. That powerful slogan, "the personal is political," addresses the connection between the self and political reality. Yet it was often interpreted as meaning that to name one's personal pain in relation to structures of domination was not just a beginning stage in the process of coming to political consciousness, to awareness, but all that was necessary. In most cases, naming one's personal pain was not sufficiently linked to overall education for critical consciousness of collective political resistance. Focussing on the personal in a framework that did not compel acknowledgement of the complexity of structures of domination could easily lead to misnaming, to the creation of yet another sophisticated level of non- or distorted awareness. This often happens in a feminist context when race and/or class are not seen as factors determining the social construction of one's gendered reality and most importantly, the extent to which one will suffer exploitation and domination.

Naming the pain or uncovering the pain in a context where it is not linked to strategies for resistance and transformation created for many women the conditions for even greater estrangement, alienation, isolation, and at times grave despair. Rather than aiding the process for self-recovery, many women felt a sense of disintegration as though their lives were becoming all the more fragmented and broken (those women who name the pain engendered by sexism and gendered oppression, who went on to emulate males and to work at assimilation into the culture of patriarchy, the culture of domination, were able to experience a sense of fulfillment denied those of us who were seeking transformation both of the self and the world around us). Longing for self-recovery, not simply the description of one's woundedness, one's victimization, or repeated discussion of the problems, many women simply became disillusioned and disinterested in feminism, uncertain about whether feminism was really a radical movement.

A complete vision of self-recovery, of the process by which the dominated and exploited individual would experience a new and different relationship to the world, was lacking. Without a doubt, contemporary feminist movement has enabled women to become more aware of the impact of sexist domination and sexist oppression in our lives. This awareness has not led masses of women to commit themselves to feminist struggle, precisely because it is not fully linked to education for critical consciousness, to collective resistance.

Awakening women to the need for change without providing substantive models and strategies for change frustrates, creates a situation where women are left with unfulfilled longings for transformation. We may know that we need transformation, we may crave transformation, but lack a sense that these desires can be addressed by feminist politics or radical politics. It is this space of longing that has come to be filled by a variety of self-help books, which offer models for personal change applicable to everyday life. Books like *Do I Think I'm Nothing Without a Man?*, *The Cinderella Complex*, *Men Are Just Desserts*, *Men Who Hate Women and the Women Who Love Them,* and the most important, the all-time favorite, *Women Who Love Too Much.*

Feminist thinking and analysis about gender roles was the radical framework legitimizing and privileging women's right to articulate problems related to gender. It provided a stimulus, a push that has unfortunately compelled many women to grasp at solutions wherever they may be found. Ironically, these very books which purport to offer the models for self-recovery that feminist work does not offer, retard and undermine both the growth of women's political consciousness and the progress of feminist movement. Within the new self-help books for women, patriarchy and male domination are rarely identified as forces that lead to the oppression, exploitation, and domination of women. Instead, these books suggest that individual relationships between men and women can be changed solely by women making the right choices. At their very core, many of these books are woman-hating. They all posit a world view in which women can be liberated solely by making right choices. This is especially true of *Women Who Love Too Much.*

This book is unique in that it is read by masses of women across race, class, and sexual preference lines. Norwood's book is appealing precisely because it addresses in an essential way the longing for self-recovery. She uses this phrase not in a radical political sense but in the way it is used in mental health circles to identify individuals working to cope with various addictions. She speaks to the pain and anguish many women feel in personal relationships, particularly the pain heterosexual women feel in relationships with men. Yet she in no way acknowledges political realities, the oppression and domination of women. Words like "male domination," "feminism," or "women's liberation" are never used, and even though she can share with readers that her husband did housework while she was writing, she shares this as though many men and most importantly, the right men, automatically assume such tasks, nurturing while women do creative work.

Just as Nancy Hartsock's new work urges us to question why we are being asked to surrender a concern with the subject at this historical moment, when women have been struggling to move from object to subject, we must ask why it is women are being seduced by models of individual change that imply that no change has to occur in larger political and social realities. We must ask ourselves why this is so appealing. Why are women willing to return to old patterns, to narratives that suggest we are responsible for male domination? As feminist activists, as feminist theorists, we must acknowledge our failure to create adequate models for radical change in everyday life that would have meaning and significance to masses of women. Until we construct and unless we construct such models, feminist movement will not have revolutionary impact transforming self and society.

6

feminist theory: a radical agenda

Any constructive examination of feminist scholarship and its political implication must necessarily focus on feminist theory. In these times of grave political and economic crisis, as we are subjected to more overt attacks by anti-feminists who either deny the validity of feminist liberation struggle or simplify the nature of that struggle, we must be actively engaged in ongoing critical dialogue about the future of feminist movement, about the direction and shape of feminist theory.

Without liberatory feminist theory, there can be no effective feminist movement. To fulfill this purpose, feminist theory must provide a structure of analysis and thought that synthesizes that which is most visionary in feminist thinking, talk, and discourse—those models of change that emerge from our understanding of sexism and sexist oppression in everyday life, coupled with strategies of resistance that effectively eradicate domination and engage us fully in a liberatory praxis.

Given this framework, feminist theory should necessarily be directed to masses of women and men in our society, educating us collectively for critical consciousness so that we can explore and understand better the workings of sexism and sexist oppression, the political basis of feminist critique, and be better able to work out strategies for resistance. Currently in the United States, the primary site for the production of feminist theory is the corporate university, and workers in this arena are primarily university educated scholars, usually from privileged race and class backgrounds with a few exceptions. Since the work of feminist theorists necessitates fundamental questioning and critiquing of the ideological structures of the prevailing white-supremacist, patriarchal hegemony, it is fitting that the university be identified as a useful site for radical political work, for feminist movement. It must be remembered that it is not and should not be the only site of such work. Academic women and men engaged in the production of feminist theory must be responsible for setting up ways to disseminate feminist thought that not only transcend the boundaries of the university setting, but that of the printed page as well. It is also our responsibility to promote and encourage the development of feminist theory by folks who are not academics. As long as the university remains "the" central site for the development of feminist scholarship, it will be necessary for us to examine the ways in which our work can be and is undermined.

Major problems with the production and dissemination of feminist theory are rooted in the various contradictions we confront within university settings. Increasingly, only one type of theory is seen as valuable—that which is Euro-centric, linguistically convoluted, and rooted in Western white male sexist and racially biased philosophical frameworks. Here I want to be clear that my criticism is not that feminist theorists focus on such work but that such work is increasingly seen as the only theory that has meaning and significance. This is problematic. Rather than expanding our notions of theory to include types of theory that can be produced in many different writing styles (hopefully we will even produce theory that begins with the experiential before it enters the printed stage), the vision of what theory is becomes a narrow, constricting concept. Rather than breaking down structures of domination, such theory is often employed to promote an academic elitism which embraces traditional structures of domination. Academics who produce theory along these lines often see themselves as superior to those who do not. Oppressive hierarchy is thus reinforced and maintained. Feminist theory is rapidly becoming another sphere of academic elitism, wherein work that is linguistically convoluted, which draws on other such works, is deemed more intellectually sophisticated, in fact is deemed more theoretical (since the stereotype of theory is that it is synonymous with that which is difficult to comprehend, linguistically convoluted) than work which is more accessible. Each time this happens, the radical, subversive potential of feminist scholarship and feminist theory in particular is undermined.

When Audre Lorde made that much quoted yet often misunderstood cautionary statement warning us that "the master's tools will never dismantle the master's house," she was urging us to remember that we must engage in a process of visionary thinking that transcends the ways of knowing privileged by the oppressive powerful if we are to truly make revolutionary change. She was, in the deep structure of this statement, reminding us that it is easy for women and any exploited or oppressed group to become complicit in structures of domination, using power in ways that reinforce rather than challenge or change. As institutional structures impose values, modes of thought, ways of being on our consciousness, those of us who work in academic settings often unwittingly become engaged in the production of a feminist theory that aims to create a new sphere of theoretical elitism. Feminist scholars who do work that is not considered theoretical or intellectually rigorous are excluded from this arena of privileged bonding. This seriously undermines feminist movement. It means that we not only lose sight of the need to produce feminist theory that is directly related to the concrete lives of women and men who are most affected by sexist oppression, but that we become engaged in an unproductive and unnecessary power struggle which deflects our critical energies and defeats our purpose.

Production and dissemination of feminist theory in forms that alienate, that cannot be understood, has promoted the continued growth of feminist anti-intellectualism and intensified the antagonism toward theory that has been pervasive throughout contemporary feminist movement. Early on, feminist educators like Charlotte Bunch emphasized the need for feminist education that would seek to alter the anti-theoretical impulse many women have learned from patriarchal conditioning. When that feminist theory deemed most valuable is articulated in a form that does not allow effective communication of ideas, it reinforces the fear, especially on the part of the exploited and oppressed, that the intent of theorizing is not to liberate but to mystify. Anti-theoretical backlash tends to privilege concrete actions and experiential resistance to sexism, however narrowly focussed their impact.

As long as university settings are the central site for the production of theory and academics are simultaneously engaged in a competitive work arena that supports and perpetuates all forms of domination, feminist theorists will need to be conscientious about not supporting monolithic notions of theory. We will need to continually assert the need for multiple theories emerging from diverse perspectives in a variety of styles. Often we simply passively accept this false dichotomy between the so called "theoretical" and that writing which appears to be more directly related to the experiential.

In many feminist theory classes, this problem is addressed by including work that is taken to represent "real life" experience or fictional portrayals of concrete reality along with work that is deemed highly theoretical. Often such attempts reinforce racism and elitism by identifying writing by working-class women and women of color as "experiential" while the writing of white women represents "theory." This past year, I saw a Women's Studies feminist theory course syllabus in which the only work by a woman of color and the only non-theoretical work was Alice Walker's novel, *The Color Purple*. Another course had a required list that included material by white women Nancy Hartsock, Zillah Eisenstein, Julia Kristeva, Alice Jardine, and then *The Color Purple*. Often novels or confessional autobiographical writings are used to mediate the tension between academic writing, theory, and the experiential. This seems to be especially the case when the issue is inclusion of works by women of color in feminist theory courses. Much of the little theoretical work done by women of color is not readily accessible—yet it can be found.

Anti-intellectual biases within feminist movement directly effect the extent to which women of color feel compelled to produce feminist theory. Many of us come from class backgrounds where intellectual activity and writing are seen as non-valuable work so we are already working to overcome this obstacle. It is profoundly disturbing to see how little feminist theory is being written by black women and other women of color. The paucity of material is not simply linked to absence of motivation; it is related to the privileging of material within feminist circles by women of color that is not only not theoretical but in some cases anti-theoretical. Why should women of color work to produce feminist theory that is likely to be ignored or devalued? How many women of color teach courses in feminist theory? Though I have done theoretical writing, I am much more likely to be asked to teach a course focussing on women and race than on theory. In those university settings where I have talked with white women who have higher rank about my desire to teach a course on feminist theory, the response is always that it is an area which is being covered already. Women of color who are theorists are devalued because of racial biases. Often our work is appropriated.

In my teaching and in my writing, I have tried, in the spirit of Charlotte Bunch (whose early writings on women and education were important precisely because they sought to encourage women not to be wary of theory), to encourage women—and particularly black women—to recognize the value and importance of theory, to acknowledge that we all use it in daily life. Theory is not an alien sphere. Even though there is much theoretical writing that may be difficult to understand, I think it useful for us not to simply dismiss or downgrade it but to talk about why it is intimidating, what possible uses it may have, and how it can be interpreted, translated, etc. so that it can be understood.

It is a disservice to black women writers and all women writers when feminist readers demand that our imaginative works serve purposes that should be addressed by feminist theory. Novels and confessional writing can and do enhance our understanding of the way individuals critically reflect about gender, the way we develop strategies to resist sexism, to change lives, but they cannot and do not take the place of theory. More importantly, it does not serve the interests of feminist movement for feminist scholars to support this unnecessary and dangerous separation of "theoretical" work and that work which focusses more on the experiential. It was disturbing to me recently to read Barbara Christian's essay, "The Race for Theory," in which she suggested again and again that black women and "people of color have always theorized—but in forms quite different from the Western form of abstract logic." This statement is simply inaccurate. Had it been made by a white person, I think many more people would be disturbed by its message. When I read it, I immediately thought about different groups of African people, like the Dogon, who have very abstract logical schemas to support rituals that focus on creating gendered subjects. I constantly tell students who use the word "abstract" to dismiss work that in everyday life we use both language and concepts that are very abstract. This point is made quite wonderfully in the collective work, *Female Sexualization*, edited by Frigga Haug who writes: "Contrary to reputation, our everyday language is more than a little abstract: it suppresses the concreteness of feelings, thoughts, and experiences, speaking of them only from a distance." Recently walking by a black male street person, I greeted him by saying, "Hi Ya' doing." And he responded, "Halfway, I'm just halfway." In my African-American literature course that day I used his comment to talk about abstraction, language, and interpretation; and the problem of assuming that "basic black people" or everyday folks do not use abstract theory. At one point, Barbara Christian writes, "I and many of my sisters do not see the world as being so simple. And perhaps that is why we have not rushed to create abstract theories."

Yes! We are not rushing to create feminist theory and I for one think that is tragic. We may not be doing so precisely because of our fears of articulating that which is abstract. All theory as I see it emerges in the realm of abstraction, even that which emerges from the most concrete of everyday experiences. My goal as a feminist thinker and theorist is to take that abstraction and articulate it in a language that renders it accessible—not less complex or rigorous—but simply more accessible.

While I agree with Barbara Christian's critique of the way in which certain types of feminist theory are not seen as an "authoritative discourse," and pointing to the dangers of that is one concern of this essay, it is important that we do not resist this hierarchical tendency by devaluing theory in general. There is a place for theory that uses convoluted language, metalanguage, yet such theory cannot become the groundwork for feminist movement unless it is more accessible. It is not uncommon for women who write theory to discount its importance when questioned about how it relates to "real life," to woman's day-to-day experience. Such dismissals reinforce the misguided assumption that all theory is and has to be inaccessible. In more recent years, focus on the experiential in some feminist circles as part of attempts to deflect attention away from theoretical work has obscured critical gaps in feminist thought and blocked awareness of the pressing need for the production of visionary feminist theory. Such theory emerges only from a context in which there is either an integration of critical thinking and concrete experience or a recognition of the way in which critical ideas, abstractly formulated, will impact on everyday life experience. Visionary feminist theory must be articulated in a manner that is accessible if it is to have meaningful impact. This is not to suggest that everyone will be able to read such work. Inability to read or write makes it impossible for masses of people to learn about written feminist theory. Literacy must become a strategic priority for feminists. Yet what cannot be read can be talked about, and talking, both in lectures and in everyday conversation, is as effective a way to share information about feminist theory as is published material. Even though the groundwork of theory may be laid in a written discourse, it need not end there.

Works of feminist scholarship and feminist theory do exist which are accessible to large numbers of readers and which can be easily discussed. To name a few: *Class and Feminism* edited by Charlotte Bunch and Nancy Myron (1974); *Women and the New World,* an anonymous pamphlet published in 1976; *Top Ranking: Essays on Racism and Classism in Lesbian Communities* edited by Joan Gibbs and Sara Bennett (1979); *Building Feminist Theory* (1981); and *The Politics of Reality: Essays in Feminist Theory* by Marilyn Frye. Most of these works would not appear on the syllabi of feminist theory courses today. In fact, with one or two exceptions, this material is out of print, hard to find, or not well known. Significantly, work within feminist theory that is difficult to comprehend is more likely to be read in theory courses, especially on the graduate level. The recent rise to prominence of a particular style of French feminist theory which is linguistically convoluted is an example of this trend. While such work enriches our understanding of gender politics, it is important to remember that this is not a universal discourse, that it is politically and culturally specific, and emerges from specific relationships particular French feminist scholars have to their political and social reality. Two thinkers whose work immediately comes to mind are Luce Irigaray (*Speculum of the Other Women*) and Julia Kristeva (*Desire in Language*). Although this work honors the relationship between feminist discourse and political practice, it is often used within university settings to establish a select intellectual elite and to reinforce and perpetuate systems of domination, most obviously white Western cultural imperialism. When any feminist theory is employed in this way, feminist movement to end sexist domination is undermined.

At this particular stage of feminist movement in the United States, feminist scholars must pause to reconsider the approach we take to our work within the university. We must be willing to critically examine anew the tensions that arise when we simultaneously try to educate in such a way as to ensure the progression of a liberatory feminist movement and work to create a respected place for feminist scholarship within academic institutions. We must also reexamine the tensions that arise when we try to subvert while working to keep jobs, to be promoted, etc. These practical concerns are factors that influence and/or determine the type of scholarship deemed important. Often, attempts to mediate or reconcile these tensions lead to frustration, despair, cooptation, complicity, or shifts in allegiance. To reaffirm the primacy of feminist struggle, feminist scholars must renew our collective commitment to a radical theoretical agenda, to a feminist education that is the practice of freedom. We begin this task by acknowledging that feminist theory is losing its vital connection to feminist struggle and that connection must be firmly reestablished and understood if our work is to have significant political impact.

7

feminist scholarship: ethical issues

When students in a course I was teaching on women and race began to discuss Bettina Aptheker's work, *Woman's Legacy: Essays on Race, Sex, and Class,* we raised the issues of whether or not white women should or should not write about black women's lives. The class was composed of thirty white students and three non-white students, three men and thirty women. A few students quickly addressed the issue by responding, "Of course, we should all write about whatever we want to write about." Other students said, "No—absolutely not—white women should not write about black women or any other group of non-white women." Many students in the class were lesbian and the majority agreed that they did not feel that non-lesbian women should write books that address lesbian experience. We talked about the fact that there was a time when almost all books written about feminist movement were written by white men, when a vast majority of books about slavery and black experience—especially academic books—were written by white people (and sometimes black men), when the few books about homosexual experience were written by non-homosexuals, relating our discussion to growing awareness that a dimension of the oppressor/oppressed, exploiter/exploited relationship is that those who dominate are seen as subjects and those who are dominated objects. As subjects, people have the right to define their own reality, establish their own identities, name their history. As objects, one's reality is defined by others, one's identity created by others, one's history named only in ways that define one's relationship to those who are subject.

We talked about the way in which every liberatory struggle initiated by groups of people who have been seen as objects begins with a revolutionary process wherein they assert that they are subjects. It is this process that Paulo Freire stresses: "we cannot enter the struggle as objects in order later to become subjects." Oppressed people resist by identifying themselves as subjects, by defining their reality, shaping their new identity, naming their history, telling their story. For white women, non-white women, black people, and all individuals from various ethnic groups who are gay, there have been historical moments wherein each of our experiences were most studied, interpreted, and written about solely by white males, or solely by a group with greater power. That group became the "authority" to consult if anyone wanted to understand the experiences of these powerless groups. This process was a manifestation of the politics of domination. It is this notion of "authority" that we began to critique and discuss in the class.

Even if perceived "authorities" writing about a group to which they do not belong and/or over which they wield power, are progressive, caring, and right-on in every way, as long as their authority is constituted by either the absence of the voices of the individuals whose experiences they seek to address, or the dismissal of those voices as unimportant, the subject-object dichotomy is maintained and domination is reinforced. In some cases, the individual who wishes to be perceived as "the authority" may go to great lengths to emphasize to readers that, for example, she is writing from her perspective as a white woman intending to diminish in no way black women's experience or our right to tell our story. Given the structure of white supremacy, her version, her take on our past may be viewed as more legitimate than similar work done by black women.

When we write about the experiences of a group to which we do not belong, we should think about the ethics of our action, considering whether or not our work will be used to reinforce and perpetuate domination. I was discussing this subject with another black woman professor and she said: "There was a time when we black people needed other people to speak for us because we could not always speak for ourselves. And though I am very grateful to white historians and the like who worked to inform people about black experience—we can and do speak for ourselves. And our struggle today is to be heard." Given the politics of domination—race, sex, and class exploitation—the tendency in this society is to place more value on what white people are writing about black people, or non-white people, rather than what we are writing about ourselves. By this comment I do not mean to suggest that white people have not written excellent books that focus on black experience; a few have. Rather, I mean that those books should not be seen as more significant and valuable than similar books by black people. Until the work of black writers and scholars is given respect and serious consideration, this overvaluation of work done by whites, which usually exists in a context wherein work done by blacks is devalued, helps maintain racism and white-supremacist attitudes.

One white Jewish student commented to me that although she had previously interpreted white Jewish intellectual study and interpretation of black experience as a sign of non-racism, of identification and concern with the political plight of black people, she had begun to see it as a sign of race and, in some cases, class privilege. She asked the class if Jewish scholars had ever encouraged black people to study and write a body of literature that purports to address and explain aspects of white Jewish experience; no one could think of an example. Yet we all agreed that if such scholarship existed in a context of diversity where black people were writing about Anglo-American experience, or Chinese-American experience, and vice-versa, there would not be the sense that such scholarship aims to maintain white supremacy. In a conversation with a Chicano historian about white scholars writing Chicano history, he mentioned a conference where a famous white male spoke of the necessity of white people writing on Chicanos so as to give the subject scholarly legitimacy, to ensure that such work would receive the proper attention, consideration, and scholarly respect. This historian could not understand that it is white-supremacist attitudes that make Chicano history more worthy of note if white people are writing it and that such "legitimation," while it may lead established white scholars to recognize the value of Chicano experience, would also perpetuate and maintain white supremacy and racist domination of Chicanos. Of course, what is negative about this situation is not that a white historian is writing about Chicano experience but the attitude toward the writing. Scholars who write about an ethnic group to which they do not belong rarely discuss in the introductions to their work the ethical issues of their race privilege, or what motivates them, or why they feel their perspective is important.

It is even more difficult for scholars who write about an ethnic group to which they do not belong to acknowledge that their work differs significantly from work done by a member of that ethnic group. Often a scholar with the same intellectual qualifications as his or her white colleague, who also has the authority of lived experience, is in the best possible position to share information about that group. When I was teaching a course called Third World Women in the United States in the Women's Studies Program at San Francisco State University, in which I endeavored to teach aspects of the history and experience of women from various ethnic groups, I was acutely conscious that my perspective, however interesting and informed, was limited. I felt that if any student in the class had the same or more advanced knowledge than myself coupled with experience of the culture we were studying that I was eager to learn from them, to abdicate my role as teacher/authority.

In crucial ways, writing about cultures or experiences of ethnic groups different from one's own becomes most political when the issue is who will be regarded as the "authoritative" voice. I can remember sitting in a classroom wherein a white woman student, who had like myself written about black slave experience, reading and studying much of the material but interpreting it differently, was seen by the white professor and classmates as the "authority" on black experience. I would make a comment about black culture and they would look to this white woman to confirm the truth or untruth of my statement. When I shared this observation, I was told that she was an "authority." What made her an authority was that her writing and training were recognized as important by white male and female academics, even though she had gleaned much of her material from black women. It did not matter to that group that she would never know what it is like to be black, to live as a black person in that very South she writes about. While I agree that her work is important, and did not feel the need to diminish it, or to suggest that it should not have been done, I felt it was important to seriously question the racist and sexist politics which determine who is an authority. White women active in feminist movement do not encourage white men to take the leading role in the making of feminist theory and scholarship, even though it is obvious that many white male academics have more experience and prestige, and one might argue are in the better position to be viewed as "authoritative voices." Yet it is acknowledged by feminist scholars that sexist biases might limit the type of work they would produce, or if they are non-sexist that their "maleness" might also serve as a barrier to understanding. This does not mean that the work of white male scholars on white women's history and sociology, etc., is not valuable. It does mean that this work is not perceived as "definitive" or the scholars themselves regarded as the most relevant voices articulating feminist thought. Yet white women who easily see the problems that arise if white males are seen as the authoritative voices within the area of scholarship about women have difficulty seeing the same issues in regards to scholarship by whites on non-white groups. Concurrently, just as racism may mean that a black woman's scholarship on black women may be seen as less than definitive, she may also receive no validation for writing on subjects that do not pertain to race or gender.

Arguing, as many feminist scholars do, against the notion of a definitive work or the very idea of "authority," can help to create a climate where scholarship from diverse groups could flourish and we would be better able to appreciate the significance of scholarship that emerges from a particular race, sex, and class perspective. In our class, we read Bettina Aptheker's *Woman's Legacy* and Grace Halsell's *Soul Sister,* and discussed both books in terms of how the authors' white, female identities may have shaped their perspectives or thoughts, highlighting the value of those perspectives while also looking at potential areas of knowledge that we felt they may have overlooked. We did the same for books by black women. Students in this course felt that if the writings by black women had not existed, there would have been a crucial gap in our understanding, that it was important to them to read black women writing about our collective history, telling stories, interpreting our experience rather than solely reading white perspectives. While these writings seemed much more relevant to the students than the writings by white women, it was important to have white perspectives for comparison and contrast, to see similarities in perspective, and differences.

Certainly it is important and necessary for people from any ethnic/racial group to play a significant role in the creation and dissemination of material about their particular experience. It is equally important for all of us to work at learning more about one another, and such learning is often best expressed in concentrated work and study on another group. I would not discourage any black student who wanted to write about the experience of Japanese-Americans in U.S. detention camps during WWII, but I would want that student to be clear about why she or he wanted to write about this subject and I would suggest careful examination to ensure that the student's perspective did not reflect racial biases. Learning about other groups and writing about what we learn can be a way to unlearn racism, to challenge structures of domination. This is especially true for scholarship non-white people do about one another. Many black people know little about Asian-American or Native American experience. Even though there are several new books about black intermingling with different Native American groups, there is no work done yet from a black perspective (that I know about), which could add so much to our understanding of that experience. When white male scholar Robert Hemenway published his biography of Zora Neale Hurston, he wrote in his introduction:

> My intention has always been simple. Zora Neale Hurston is a literary artist of sufficient talent to deserve intensive study, both as an artist and as an intellect. She deserves an important place in American literary history. I have tried to demonstrate why this is so, not in the interest of producing a "definitive" book—that book remains to be written, and by a black woman—but in order to provide a new, closer examination of the unusual career of this complex author.

As a black female literary critic, I have always appreciated this statement, not because I share the notion of "definitive" works, but because I share the sense that a black woman might write about Hurston in ways that would illuminate her writing that would be radically different from that of other scholars. By actively refusing the position of "authority," Hemenway encourages black women to participate in the making of Hurston scholarship and allows for the possibility that a black woman writing about Hurston may have special insight.

On the first day of my class on Contemporary Black Women Novelists, a class in which all the students were white, students expressed discomfort that there were no black women in the class, and then other students expressed similar feelings. When I asked them to explain why this disturbed them, they responded by saying that it seemed a bit ludicrous for them to be listening to one another talk about black women's fiction, that they would probably say stupid, racist things, and that they wanted to hear from black women. While I think it a meaningful gesture for young white women in a white-supremacist culture to seek to hear from black women, to wish to listen and learn from black women, I cautioned them against turning the spheres of discussion on racial topics (or in this case, black women's writing) into yet another arena where we as black people are called upon to take primary responsibility for sharing experiences, ideas, and information. Such a gesture places black people once again in a service position, meeting the needs of whites. I stressed that the ideal situation for learning is always one where there is diversity and dialogue, where there would be women and men from various groups. But I also insisted that we should all be capable of learning about an ethnic/racial group and studying its literature even if no person from that group is present. I told students that I did not think that I needed to be a white man to understand Hemingway's *The Sun Also Rises* nor did I think I needed to be in a classroom with white men to study this novel. However, I do recognize that as a black woman reading this white male writer I might have insights and interpretations that would be quite different from those of white male readers who might approach the text with the assumption that the novel's depiction of white male social reality was one they shared. I would, however, consider my insights equally valuable, just as I thought my students should see their insights about black women's fiction as valuable even though the discussion might be more complex and interesting if those insights were shared in a context with black women's ideas.

I shared with this class a concern about the way in which recent feminist focus on differences, especially racial differences, has led to a sense that white women must abdicate responsibility for responding to works by "different others." I was disturbed when I read Joanna Russ' book *How to Suppress Women's Writing,* where she continually stressed the importance of literature by women of color by saying that she did not feel that as a white woman scholar she was in a position to speak about these works. Toward the end of the book, she listed many quotes from works by women of color ostensibly encouraging readers to read these writers, to see their words as important. Yet this gesture disturbed me because it also implied that women of color represent this group whose experiences and whose writing is so removed from that of white women that they cannot address such work critically and analytically. This assumption may very well reinforce racism. It helps (as white students in class pointed out) take the burden of accountability away from white women and places it solely onto women of color. While I recognize that there are probably women of color who feel it is appropriate for Russ to assume such a passive position, not asserting her thoughts about black women's literature, I would have appreciated hearing those thoughts. I would have appreciated a sentence that might have begun, "As a white woman reading Toni Morrison's *Sula*, I was..." Such a position would allow white women scholars to share their ideas about black women's writing (or any group of women's writing) without assuming that their thoughts would be seen as "definitive" or that they would be trying to be "the authority." Again, I can only reiterate a point made throughout this piece, that problems arise not when white women choose to write about the experiences of non-white people, but when such material is presented as "authoritative."

Cross-ethnic feminist scholarship should emphasize the value of a scholar's work as well as the unique perspective that scholar brings to bear on the subject. I do not wish for a situation where only black women are encouraged to write about issues related to black female experience. I do, however, wish to help make a world wherein scholarship and work by black women is valued so that we will be motivated to do such work, so that our voices will be heard. I wish to help make a world where our work will be taken seriously, given appreciation, and acclaimed, a world in which such work will be seen as necessary and significant.

8

toward a revolutionary feminist pedagogy

My favorite teacher in high school was Miss Annie Mae Moore, a short, stout black woman. She had taught my mama and her sisters. She could tell story after story about their fast ways, their wildness. She could tell me ways I was like mama, ways I was most truly my own self. She could catch hold of you and turn you around, set you straight (these were the comments folk made about her teaching)—so that we would know what we were facing when we entered her classroom. Passionate in her teaching, confident that her work in life was a pedagogy of liberation (words she would not have used but lived instinctively), one that would address and confront our realities as black children growing up in the segregated South, black children growing up within a white-supremacist culture. Miss Moore knew that if we were to be fully self-realized, then her work, and the work of all our progressive teachers, was not to teach us solely the knowledge in books, but to teach us an oppositional world view—different from that of our exploiters and oppressors, a world view that would enable us to see ourselves not through the lens of racism or racist stereotypes but one that would enable us to focus clearly and succinctly, to look at ourselves, at the world around us, critically—analytically—to see ourselves first and foremost as striving for wholeness, for unity of heart, mind, body, and spirit.

It was as a student in segregated black schools called Booker T. Washington and Crispus Attucks that I witnessed the transformative power of teaching, of pedagogy. In particular, those teachers who approached their work as though it was indeed a pedagogy, a science of teaching, requiring diverse strategies, approaches, explorations, experimentation, and risks, demonstrated the value—the political power—of teaching. Their work was truly education for critical consciousness. In these segregated schools, the teachers were almost all black women. Many of them had chosen teaching at a historical moment when they were required by custom to remain single and childless, to have no visible erotic or sexual life. Among them were exceptional teachers who gave to their work a passion, a devotion that made it seem a true calling, a true vocation. They were the teachers who conceptualized oppositional world views, who taught us young black women to exult and glory in the power and beauty of our intellect. They offered to us a legacy of liberatory pedagogy that demanded active resistance and rebellion against sexism and racism. They embodied in their work, in their lives (for none of them appeared as tortured spinsters estranged and alienated from the world around them) a feminist spirit. They were active participants in black community, shaping our futures, mapping our intellectual terrains, sharing revolutionary fervor and vision. I write these words, this essay to express the honor and respect I have for them because they have been my pedagogical guardians. Their work has had a profound impact on my consciousness, on my development as a teacher.

During years of graduate school, I waited for that phase of study when we would focus on the meaning and significance of pedagogy, when we would learn about teaching, about how to teach. That moment never arrived. For years I have relied on those earlier models of excellent teaching to guide me. Most specifically, I understood from the teachers in those segregated schools that the work of any teacher committed to the full self-realization of students was necessarily and fundamentally radical, that ideas were not neutral, that to teach in a way that liberates, that expands consciousness, that awakens, is to challenge domination at its very core. It is this pedagogy that Paulo Freire calls "education as the practice of freedom." In his introduction to Freire's *Pedagogy of the Oppressed*, Richard Shaull writes:

> Education either functions as an instrument which is used to facilitate the integration of the younger generation into the logic of the present system and bring about conformity to it, or it becomes "the practice of freedom," the means by which men and women deal critically and creatively with reality and discover how to participate in the transformation of their world.

A liberatory feminist movement aims to transform society by eradicating patriarchy, by ending sexism and sexist oppression, by challenging the politics of domination on all fronts. Feminist pedagogy can only be liberatory if it is truly revolutionary because the mechanisms of appropriation within white-supremacist, capitalist patriarchy are able to co-opt with tremendous ease that which merely appears radical or subversive. Within the United States, contemporary feminist movement is sustained in part by the efforts academic women make to constitute the university setting as a central site for the development and dissemination of feminist thought. Women's Studies has been the location of this effort. Given the way universities work to reinforce and perpetuate the status quo, the way knowledge is offered as commodity, Women's Studies can easily become a place where revolutionary feminist thought and feminist activism are submerged or made secondary to the goals of academic careerism. Without diminishing in any way our struggle as academics striving to succeed in institutions, such effort is fully compatible with liberatory feminist struggle only when we consciously, carefully, and strategically link the two. When this connection is made initially but not sustained, or when it is never evident, Women's Studies becomes either an exotic terrain for those politically chic few seeking affirmation or a small settlement within the larger institutional structure where women (and primarily white women) have a power base, which rather than being oppositional simply mirrors the status quo. When feminist struggle is the central foundation for feminist education, Women's Studies and the feminist classroom (which can exist outside the domain of Women's Studies) can be places where education is the practice of freedom, the place for liberatory pedagogy.

At this historical moment, there is a crisis of engagement within universities, for when knowledge becomes commoditized, then much authentic learning ceases. Students who want to learn hunger for a space where they can be challenged intellectually. Students also suffer, as many of us who teach do, from a crisis of meaning, unsure about what has value in life, unsure even about whether it is important to stay alive. They long for a context where their subjective needs can be integrated with study, where the primary focus is a broader spectrum of ideas and modes of inquiry, in short a dialectical context where there is serious and rigorous critical exchange. This is an important and exciting time for feminist pedagogy because in theory and practice our work meets these needs.

Feminist education—the feminist classroom—is and should be a place where there is a sense of struggle, where there is visible acknowledgement of the union of theory and practice, where we work together as teachers and students to overcome the estrangement and alienation that have become so much the norm in the contemporary university. Most importantly, feminist pedagogy should engage students in a learning process that makes the world "more rather than less real." In my classrooms, we work to dispel the notion that our experience is not a "real world" experience. This is especially easy since gender is such a pressing issue in contemporary life. Every aspect of popular culture alerts us to the reality that folks are thinking about gender in both reactionary and progressive ways. What is important is that they are thinking critically. And it is this space that allows for the possibility of feminist intervention, whether it be in our classroom or in the life of students outside the classroom. Lately, there has been a truly diverse body of students coming to my classes and other feminist classes at universities all around the United States. Many of us have been wondering "what's going on" or "why are all these men, and white men in the class." This changing student body reflects the concern about gender issues, that it is one of the real important issues in people's private lives that is addressed academically. Freire writes, "Education as the practice of freedom—as opposed to education as the practice of domination—denies that we are abstract, isolated, independent, and unattached to the world; it also denies that the world exists as a reality apart from us."

To make a revolutionary feminist pedagogy, we must relinquish our ties to traditional ways of teaching that reinforce domination. This is very difficult. Women's Studies courses are often viewed as not seriously academic because so much "personal stuff" is discussed. Fear that their courses will be seen as "gut" classes has led many feminist professors to rely more on traditional pedagogical styles. This is unfortunate. Certainly, the radical alternative to the status quo should never have been simply an inversion. That is to say, critical of the absence of any focus on personal experience in traditional classrooms, such focus becomes the central characteristic of the feminist classroom. This model must be viewed critically because a class can still be reinforcing domination, not transforming consciousness about gender, even as the "personal" is the ongoing topic of conversation.

To have a revolutionary feminist pedagogy we must first focus on the teacher-student relationship and the issue of power. How do we as feminist teachers use power in a way that is not coercive, dominating? Many women have had difficulty asserting power in the feminist classroom for fear that to do so would be to exercise domination. Yet we must acknowledge that our role as teacher is a position of power over others. We can use that power in ways that diminish or in ways that enrich and it is this choice that should distinguish feminist pedagogy from ways of teaching that reinforce domination. One simple way to alter the way one's "power" as teacher is experienced in the classroom is to elect not to assume the posture of all-knowing professors. This is also difficult. When we acknowledge that we do not know everything, that we do not have all the answers, we risk students leaving our classrooms and telling others that we are not prepared. It is important to make it clear to students that we are prepared and that the willingness to be open and honest about what we do no know is a gesture of respect for them.

To be oppositional in the feminist classroom one must have a standard of valuation that differs from the norm. Many of us tried new ways of teaching without changing the standards by which we evaluated our work. We often left the classroom feeling uncertain about the learning process or even concerned that we were failing as teachers. Let me share a particular problem I have faced. My classroom style is very confrontational. It is a model of pedagogy that is based on the assumption that many students will take courses from me who are afraid to assert themselves as critical thinkers, who are afraid to speak (especially students from oppressed and exploited groups). The revolutionary hope that I bring to the classroom is that it will become a space where they can come to voice. Unlike the stereotypical feminist model that suggests women best come to voice in an atmosphere of safety (one in which we are all going to be kind and nurturing), I encourage students to work at coming to voice in an atmosphere where they may be afraid or see themselves at risk. The goal is to enable all students, not just an assertive few, to feel empowered in a rigorous, critical discussion. Many students find this pedagogy difficult, frightening, and very demanding. They do not usually come away from my class talking about how much they enjoyed the experience.

One aspect of traditional models of teaching I had not surrendered was that longing for immediate recognition of my value as a teacher, and immediate affirmation. Often I did not feel liked or affirmed and this was difficult for me to accept. I reflected on my student experiences and the reality that I often learned the most in classes that I did not enjoy and complained about, which helped me to work on the traditional assumption that immediate positive feedback is the signifier of worth. Concurrently, I found that students who often felt they hated a class with me would return later to say how much they learned, that they understood that it was the different style that made it hard as well as the different demands. I began to see that courses that work to shift paradigms, to change consciousness, cannot necessarily be experienced immediately as fun or positive or safe and this was not a worthwhile criteria to use in evaluation.

In the feminist classroom, it is important to define the terms of engagement, to identify what we mean when we say that a course will be taught from a feminist perspective. Often the initial explanations about pedagogy will have a serious impact on the way students experience a course. It is important to talk about pedagogical strategy. For a time, I assumed that students would just get the hang of it, would see that I was trying to teach in a different way and accept it without explanation. Often, that meant I explained after being criticized. It is important for feminist professors to explain not only what will differ about the classroom experience but to openly acknowledge that students must consider whether they wish to be in such a learning space. On a basic level, students are often turned off by the fact that I take attendance, but because I see the classroom experience as constituting a unique learning experience, to miss class is to really lose a significant aspect of the process. Whether or not a student attends class affects grading and this bothers students who are not accustomed to taking attendance seriously. Another important issue for me has been that each student participate in classroom discussion, that each student have a voice.

This is a practice I think is important not because every student has something valuable to say (this is not always so), but often students who do have meaningful comments to contribute are silent. In my classes, everyone's voice is heard as students read paragraphs which may explore a particular issue. They do not have the opportunity to refuse to read paragraphs. When I hear their voices, I become more aware of information they may not know that I can provide. Whether a class is large or small, I try to talk with all students individually or in small groups so that I have a sense of their needs. How can we transform consciousness if we do not have some sense of where the students are intellectually, psychically?

Concern with how and what students are learning validates and legitimates a focus, however small, on personal confession in classroom discussions. I encourage students to relate the information they are learning to the personal identities they are working to socially construct, to change, to affirm. If the goal of personal confession is not narcissism, it must take place within a critical framework where it is related to material that is being discussed. When, for example, I am teaching Toni Morrison's novel, *The Bluest Eye*, I may have students write personal paragraphs about the relationship between race and physical beauty, which they read in class. Their paragraphs may reveal pain, woundedness as they explore and express ways they are victimized by racism and sexism, or they may express ideas that are racist and sexist. Yet the paragraphs enable them to approach the text in a new way. They may read the novel differently. They may be able to be more critical and analytical. If this does not happen, then the paragraphs fail as a pedagogical tool. To make feminist classrooms the site of transformative learning experiences, we must constantly try new methods, new approaches.

Finally, we cannot have a revolutionary feminist pedagogy if we do not have revolutionary feminists in the classroom. Women's Studies courses must do more than offer a different teaching style; we must really challenge issues of sexism and sexist oppression both by what we teach and how we teach. This is truly a collective effort. We must learn from one another, sharing ideas and pedagogical strategies. Although I have invited feminist colleagues to come and participate in my classes, they do not. Classroom territoriality is another traditional taboo. Yet if we are to learn from one another, if we are to develop a concrete strategy for radicalizing our classrooms, we must be more engaged as a group. We must be willing to deconstruct this power dimension, to challenge, change, and create new approaches. If we are to move toward a revolutionary feminist pedagogy, we must challenge ourselves and one another to restore to feminist struggle its radical and subversive dimension. We must be willing to restore the spirit of risk—to be fast, wild, to be able to take hold, turn around, transform.

9

black and female: reflections on graduate school

I Searching for material to read in a class about women and race, I found an essay in *Heresies: Racism is the Issue* that fascinated me. I realized that it was one of the first written discussions of the struggles black English majors (and particularly black women) face when we study at predominately white universities. The essay, "On Becoming A Feminist Writer," is by Carole Gregory. She begins by explaining that she has been raised in racially segregated neighborhoods but that no one had ever really explained "white racism or white male sexism." Psychically, she was not prepared to confront head-on these aspects of social reality, yet they were made visible as soon as she registered for classes:

> Chewing on a brown pipe, a white professor said, "English departments do not hire Negroes or women!" Like a guillotine, his voice sought to take my head off. Racism in my hometown was an economic code of etiquette which stifled Negroes and women.
>
> "If you are supposed to explain these courses, that's all I want," I answered. Yet I wanted to kill this man. Only my conditioning as a female kept me from striking his volcanic red face. My murderous impulses were raging.

Her essay chronicles her struggles to pursue a discipline which interests her without allowing racism or sexism to defeat and destroy her intellectual curiosity, her desire to teach. The words of this white male American Literature professor echo in her mind years later when she finds employment difficult, when she confronts the reality that black university teachers of English are rare. Although she is writing in 1982, she concludes her essay with the comment:

> Many years ago, an American literature professor had cursed the destiny of "Negroes and women." There was truth in his ugly words. Have you ever had a Black woman for an English teacher in the North? Few of us are able to earn a living. For the past few years, I have worked as an adjunct in English. Teaching brings me great satisfaction; starving does not.... I still remember the red color of the face which said, "English departments do not hire Negroes or women." Can women change this indictment? These are the fragments I add to my journal.

Reading Carole Gregory's essay, I recalled that in all my years of studying in English department classes, I had never been taught by a black woman. In my years of teaching, I have encountered students both in English classes and other disciplines who have never been taught by black women. Raised in segregated schools until my sophomore year of high school, I had wonderful black women teachers as role models. It never occurred to me that I would not find them in university classrooms. Yet I studied at four universities—Stanford, University of Wisconsin, University of Southern California, and the University of California, Santa Cruz—and I did not once have the opportunity to study with a black woman English professor. They were never members of the faculty. I considered myself lucky to study with one black male professor at Stanford who was visiting and another at the University of Southern California even though both were reluctant to support and encourage black female students. Despite their sexism and internalized racism, I appreciated them as teachers and felt they affirmed that black scholars could teach literature, could work in English departments. They offered a degree of support and affirmation, however relative, that countered the intense racism and sexism of many white professors.

Changing hiring practices have meant that there are increasingly more black professors in predominately white universities, but their presence only mediates in a minor way the racism and sexism of white professors. During my graduate school years, I dreaded talking face-to-face with white professors, especially white males. I had not developed this dread as an undergraduate because there it was simply assumed that black students, and particularly black female students, were not bright enough to make it in graduate school. While these racist and sexist opinions were rarely directly stated, the message was conveyed through various humiliations that were aimed at shaming students, at breaking our spirit. We were terrorized. As an undergraduate, I carefully avoided those professors who made it clear that the presence of any black students in their classes was not desired.

Unlike Carole Gregory's first encounter, they did not make direct racist statements. Instead, they communicated their message in subtle ways—forgetting to call your name when reading the roll, avoiding looking at you, pretending they do not hear you when you speak, and at times ignoring you altogether.

The first time this happened to me I was puzzled and frightened. It was clear to me and all the other white students that the professor, a white male, was directing aggressive mistreatment solely at me. These other students shared with me that it was not likely that I would pass the class no matter how good my work, that the professor would find something wrong with it. They never suggested that this treatment was informed by racism and sexism; it was just that the professor had for whatever "unapparent" reason decided to dislike me. Of course, there were rare occasions when taking a course meant so much to me that I tried to confront racism, to talk with the professor; and there were required courses. Whenever I tried to talk with professors about racism, they always denied any culpability. Often I was told, "I don't even notice that you are black."

In graduate school, it was especially hard to choose courses that would not be taught by professors who were quite racist. Even though one could resist by naming the problem and confronting the person, it was rarely possible to find anyone who could take such accusations seriously. Individual white professors were supported by white-supremacist institutions, by racist colleagues, by hierarchies that placed the word of the professor above that of the student. When I would tell the more supportive professors about racist comments that were said behind closed doors, during office hours, there would always be an expression of disbelief, surprise, and suspicion about the accuracy of what I was reporting. Mostly they listened because they felt it was their liberal duty to do so. Their disbelief, their refusal to take responsibility for white racism made it impossible for them to show authentic concern or help. One professor of 18th century literature by white writers invited me to his office to tell me that he would personally see to it that I would never receive a graduate degree. I, like many other students in the class, had written a paper in a style that he disapproved of, yet only I was given this response. It was often in the very areas of British and American literature where racism abounds in the texts studied that I would encounter racist individuals.

Gradually, I began to shift my interest in early American literature to more modern and contemporary works. This shift was influenced greatly by an encounter with a white male professor of American literature whose racism and sexism was unchecked. In his classes, I, as well as other students, was subjected to racist and sexist jokes. Any of us that he considered should not be in graduate school were the objects of particular scorn and ridicule. When we gave oral presentations, we were told our work was stupid, pathetic, and were not allowed to finish. If we resisted in any way, the situation worsened. When I went to speak with him about his attitude,

I was told that I was not really graduate school material, that I should drop out. My anger surfaced and I began to shout, to cry. I remember yelling wildly, "Do you love me? And if you don't love me then how can you have any insight about my concerns and abilities? And who are you to make such suggestions on the basis of one class." He of course was not making a suggestion. His was a course one had to pass to graduate. He was telling me that I could avoid the systematic abuse by simply dropping out. I would not drop out. I continued to work even though it was clear that I would not succeed, even as the persecution became more intense. And even though I constantly resisted.

In time, my spirits were more and more depressed. I began to dream of entering the professor's office with a loaded gun. There I would demand that he listen, that he experience the fear, the humiliation. In my dreams I could hear his pleading voice begging me not to shoot, to remain calm. As soon as I put the gun down he would become his old self again. Ultimately in the dream the only answer was to shoot, to shoot to kill. When this dream became so consistently a part of my waking fantasies, I knew that it was time for me to take a break from graduate school. Even so I felt as though his terrorism had succeeded, that he had indeed broken my spirit. It was this feeling that led me to return to graduate school, to his classes, because I felt I had given him too much power over me and I needed to regain that sense of self and personal integrity that I allowed him to diminish. Through much of my graduate school career, I was told that "I did not have the proper demeanor of a graduate student." In one graduate program, the black woman before me, who was also subjected to racist and sexist aggression, would tell me that they would say she was not as smart as me but she knew her place. I did not know my place. Young white radicals began to use the phrase "student as nigger" precisely to call attention to the way in which hierarchies within universities encouraged domination of the powerless by the powerful. At many universities the proper demeanor of a graduate student is exemplary when that student is obedient, when he or she does not challenge or resist authority.

During graduate school, white students would tell me that it was important not to question, challenge, or resist. Their tolerance level seemed much higher than my own or that of other black students. Critically reflecting on the differences between us, it was apparent that many of the white students were from privileged class backgrounds. Tolerating the humiliations and degradations we were subjected to in graduate school did not radically call into question their integrity, their sense of self-worth. Those of us who were coming from underprivileged class backgrounds, who were black, often were able to attend college only because we had consistently defied those who had attempted to make us believe we were smart but not "smart enough"; guidance counselors who refused to tell us about certain colleges because they already knew we would not be accepted; parents who were not necessarily supportive of graduate work, etc. White students were not living daily in a world outside campus life where they also had to resist degradation, humiliation. To them, tolerating forms of exploitation and domination in graduate school did not evoke images of a lifetime spent tolerating abuse. They would endure certain forms of domination and abuse, accepting it as an initiation process that would conclude when they became the person in power. In some ways they regarded graduate school and its many humiliations as a game, and they submitted to playing the role of subordinate. I and many other students, especially non-white students from non-privileged backgrounds, were unable to accept and play this "game." Often we were ambivalent about the rewards promised. Many of us were not seeking to be in a position of power over others. Though we wished to teach, we did not want to exert coercive authoritarian rule over others. Clearly those students who played the game best were usually white males and they did not face discrimination, exploitation, and abuse in many other areas of their lives.

Many black graduate students I knew were concerned about whether we were striving to participate in structures of domination and were uncertain about whether we could assume positions of authority. We could not envision assuming oppressive roles. For some of us, failure, failing, being failed began to look like a positive alternative, a way out, a solution. This was especially true for those students who felt they were suffering mentally, who felt that they would never be able to recover a sense of wholeness or well-being. In recent years, campus awareness of the absence of support for international students who have many conflicts and dilemmas in an environment that does not acknowledge their cultural codes has led to the development of support networks. Yet there has been little recognition that there are black students and other non-white students who suffer similar problems, who come from backgrounds where we learned different cultural codes. For example, we may learn that it is important not to accept coercive authoritarian rule from someone who is not a family elder—hence we may have difficulties accepting strangers assuming such a role.

Not long ago, I was at a small party with faculty from a major liberal California university, which until recently had no black professors in the English department who were permanent staff, though they were sometimes visiting scholars. One non-white faculty member and myself began to talk about the problems facing black graduate students studying in English departments. We joked about the racism within English departments, commenting that other disciplines were slightly more willing to accept study of the lives and works of non-white people yet such work is rarely affirmed in English departments where the study of literature usually consists of many works by white men and a few by white women. We talked about how some departments were struggling to change. Speaking about his department, he commented that they have only a few black graduate students, sometimes none, that at one time two black students, one male and one female, had been accepted and both had serious mental health problems. At departmental meetings, white faculty suggested that this indicated that black students just did not have the wherewithal to succeed in this graduate program. For a time, no black students were admitted. His story revealed that part of the burden these students may have felt, which many of us have felt, is that our performance will have future implications for all black students and this knowledge heightens one's performance anxiety from the very beginning. Unfortunately, racist biases often lead departments to see the behavior of one black student as an indication of the way all black students will perform academically. Certainly, if individual white students have difficulty adjusting or succeeding within a graduate program, it is not seen as an indication that all other white students will fail.

The combined forces of racism and sexism often make the black female graduate experience differ in kind from that of the black male experience. While he may be subjected to racial biases, his maleness may serve to mediate the extent to which he will be attacked, dominated, etc. Often it is assumed that black males are better able to succeed at graduate school in English than black females. While many white scholars may be aware of a black male intellectual tradition, they rarely know about black female intellectuals. African-American intellectual traditions, like those of white people, have been male-dominated. People who know the names of W.E.B. Dubois or Martin Delaney may have never heard of Mary Church Terrell or Anna Cooper. The small numbers of black women in permanent positions in academic institutions do not constitute a significant presence, one strong enough to challenge racist and sexist biases. Often the only black woman white professors have encountered is a domestic worker in their home. Yet there are no sociological studies that I know of which examine whether a group who has been seen as not having intellectual capability will automatically be accorded respect and recognition if they enter positions that suggest they are representative scholars. Often black women are such an "invisible presence" on campuses that many students may not be aware that any black women teach at the universities they attend.

Given the reality of racism and sexism, being awarded advanced degrees does not mean that black women will achieve equity with black men or other groups in the profession. Full-time, non-white women comprise less than 3 percent of the total faculty on most campuses. Racism and sexism, particularly on the graduate level, shape and influence both the academic performance and employment of black female academics. During my years of graduate work in English, I was often faced with the hostility of white students who felt that because I was black and female I would have no trouble finding a job. This was usually the response from professors as well if I expressed fear of not finding employment. Ironically, no one ever acknowledged that we were never taught by any of these black women who were taking all the jobs. No one wanted to see that perhaps racism and sexism militate against the hiring of black women even though we are seen as a group that will be given priority, preferential status. Such assumptions, which are usually rooted in the logic of affirmative action hiring, do not include recognition of the ways most universities do not strive to attain diversity of faculty and that often diversity means hiring one non-white person, one black person. When I and other black women graduate students surveyed English departments in the United States, we did not see masses of black women and rightly felt concerned about our futures.

Moving around often, I attended several graduate schools but finally finished my work at the University of California, Santa Cruz where I found support despite the prevalence of racism and sexism. Since I had much past experience, I was able to talk with white faculty members before entering the program about whether they would be receptive and supportive of my desire to focus on African-American writers. I was given positive reassurance that proved accurate. More and more, there are university settings where black female graduate students and black graduate students can study in supportive atmospheres. Racism and sexism are always present yet they do not necessarily shape all areas of graduate experience. When I talk with black female graduate students working in English departments, I hear that many of the problems have not changed, that they experience the same intense isolation and loneliness that characterized my experience. This is why I think it is important that black women in higher education write and talk about our experiences, about survival strategies. When I was having a very difficult time, I read *Working It Out*. Despite the fact that the academics who described the way in which sexism had shaped their academic experience in graduate school were white women, I was encouraged by their resistance, by their perseverance, by their success. Reading their stories helped me to feel less alone. I wrote this essay because of the many conversations I have had with black female graduate students who despair, who are frustrated, who are fearful that the experiences they are having are unique. I want them to know that they are not alone, that the problems that arise, the obstacles created by racism and sexism are real—that they do exist—they do hurt but they are not insurmountable. Perhaps these words will give solace, will intensify their courage, and renew their spirit.

10

on being black at yale: education as the practice of freedom

We lived in the country where roads were not paved, where the dust settled on our legs, which were freshly washed and adorned with grease, where we could strut and shake in the middle of the street so few cars passed our way. Every day it seemed we complained about the long walk to the little white wood frame schoolhouse and our father told us again and again about the many miles he had walked to attend school. We wanted to shut out his words—his experience. They kept coming back, returning as we grew—as we learned that education for black folks was hard to come by, was struggle, was necessary—a way to be free. Generations of black people have known what it means to see education as the practice of freedom. Though I own these words today, which first entered my consciousness through the work of Brazilian educator Paulo Freire, comrade and teacher, their meaning has always been in my life, in my experience. Growing up in a community where I would be sent here and there to read the Bible to Miss Zula because she does not know how, to read this and that, a letter, words on a detergent box—to read—to write for others. How could I not understand the need for literacy? How could I not long to know? And how could I forget that fundamentally the purpose of my knowing was so I could serve those who did not know, so that I could learn and teach my own—education as the practice of freedom.

Generations of black Americans living in a white-supremacist country have known what it means to see education as the practice of freedom, have known what it means to educate for critical consciousness. In his 1845 slave narrative, Frederick Douglass, whose papers are here at Yale, cites a white master's insistence that learning to read would make him unfit to be a slave as a moment of critical awakening:

> It was a new and special revelation, explaining dark and mysterious things, with which my youthful understanding had struggled, but struggled in vain....From that moment, I understood the pathway from slavery to freedom.

In these contemporary times, literacy remains a crucial issue—a right many black people struggle to obtain, even as more black people than ever before have the opportunity not just to read and write but to become learned women and men, academics, intellectuals. Despite civil rights struggle, the many reforms that have made it possible for us to study and teach at universities throughout the United States, we continue to live in a white-supremacist country. While we no longer live within the rigid structures of racial apartheid that characterized earlier moments in our history, we live within a culture of domination, surrounded by institutions—religious, educational, etc.—which reinforce the values, beliefs, and underlying assumptions of white supremacy. More than ever before educated black people internalize many of these assumptions, acting in complicity with the very forces of domination that actively oppress, exploit, and deny the vast majority of us access to a life that is not marred by brutal poverty, dehumanization, extreme alienation, and despair.

Black academics are not individually confronted daily with the horrendous acts of racial discrimination and exploitation that once served as constant reminders that the struggle to end racist domination could not cease—that our lot remains intimately connected with the fate of all oppressed black people, in the United States and globally. This has led many black scholars to become unmindful of the radical traditions established by black educators who were deeply committed to transforming society, who were not concerned solely with individual progress or simply transmitting facts about a particular discipline.

Yale is one of the many universities in the United States where significant radical political effort to transform the institution both in terms of the racial make-up of students and faculty and in terms of perspectives on knowledge and reality is either no longer remembered or deemed unimportant. Failure to continue and promote such effort not only inhibits the likelihood that the vision of academic freedom that has illuminated the hearts and minds of scholars here can ever be fully realized; it promotes

an atmosphere of demoralization, alienation, and despair among concerned, aware students and faculty, especially black students and faculty.
Irrespective of our political perspectives, specific academic pursuits, or personal lifestyles, black scholars at Yale, both students and faculty, confront
the question of race in one way or another—in the form of our very
presence here. Do we belong? Is our equality of intelligence and skill recognized? Do we believe solidarity is important? Are we serving the interests
of black liberation? Do we value education as the practice of freedom?

A central concern for me as teacher and scholar is this last issue—
education as the practice of freedom. If black scholars are actively committed to a liberatory pedagogy then that concern shapes and informs all
other perceptions of our role. It is a concern rooted in the awareness of
political reality, especially the circumstances of oppressed groups, a concern which compels recognition of the ways in which institutions of higher
education have been structured so that knowledge is used in the service
of maintaining white supremacy and other forms of domination, a concern
which compels us to confront the reality that education is not a neutral
process. Emphasizing this very point in his introduction to Freire's *Pedagogy of the Oppressed*, Richard Shaull asserts:

> Education either functions as an instrument which is used to facilitate
> the integration of the younger generation into the logic of the present
> system and bring about conformity to it, or it becomes "the practice
> of freedom," the means by which men and women deal critically and
> creatively with reality and discover how to participate in the transfor-
> mation of the world.

Often scholars who are deeply committed to realizing the vision of
academic freedom are the most reluctant to acknowledge that education
is not a neutral process. They become disturbed when classroom discussions take on an overtly political tone even though they may not be disturbed by course syllabi which promote and perpetuate white supremacy.
In his inaugural address at Yale, Benno Schmidt stated that, "The central
mission of a university is to preserve, disseminate, and advance knowledge
through teaching and research." He continued, "The foundation of this mission is academic freedom and absolute adherence to freedom of expression within the University and the associated freedoms and protections that
sustain it." Again and again, academic freedom is evoked to deflect attention away from the ways knowledge is used to reinforce and perpetuate
domination, away from the ways in which education is not a neutral
process. Whenever this happens, the very idea of academic freedom loses
its meaning and integrity.

This issue is especially relevant to black scholars. We too have been
seduced by the false assumption that the goal of academic freedom is best
served by postures of political neutrality, by teaching methods that belie
the reality that our very choice of subject matter, manner, and style of

presentation embodies ideological and political signifiers. Assuming this posture, there are black professors at Yale and other universities who feel it essential that they do not call attention to race and/or racism, who feel that they should behave always in a manner that deemphasizes race. This is extremely tragic. Such behavior in no way serves the interest of academic freedom. Instead it participates in the construction of a social reality wherein conformity to a racist, white male norm of representation prevails, where difference and diversity are assaulted, denied place and value. Academic freedom is most fully and truly realized when there is diversity of intellectual representation and perspective. Racism has always threatened the realization of this ideal. Rather than become accomplices in the perpetuation of racial domination, black scholars who value academic freedom must continually work to establish spheres of learning in institutions where intellectual practice is not informed by white supremacy. If such a place cannot or does not exist, we betray the radical traditions that enabled us to enter these institutions and act in a manner that will uphold and support our exclusion in the future. It is our collective responsibility both to ourselves as black people and to the academic communities in which we participate and to which we belong, to assume a primary role in establishing and maintaining academic and social spaces wherein the principles of education as the practice of freedom are promoted.

Currently, we are called by alarming circumstance—resurgence of overt racist violence, increasing deprivation and poverty, widespread illiteracy, and overwhelming psychological devastation which produces madness across all boundaries of class—to critically examine and reevaluate our role as black scholars. We must ask ourselves how it can be that many of us lack critical consciousness, have little or no understanding of the politics of race, deny that white supremacy threatens our existence and well-being, and act in complicity by internalizing racism and denigrating and devaluing blackness. We must identify the ways these assumptions, beliefs, and values are expressed so as to construct strategies of resistance and transformation. Most importantly, we must call attention to those aspects of black experience here at Yale—educational and social—where blackness is affirmed, where education as the practice of freedom is expressed.

When I applied to Yale for a teaching job, I did so because the position was a joint appointment in African-American Studies. I would not have accepted a job solely in the English Department. I believed that I would find in African-American Studies a place within the university wherein scholarship focussing on black people would be unequivocally deemed valuable—as necessary a part of the production of knowledge as all other work. I believed that I would also find support for any work I might choose to do as a black scholar that did not focus on black people. It is a testament to the struggle and commitment of black scholars here at Yale, past and present, who worked to establish African-American Studies, that however ravaged by time and circumstance, it continues to be just such a place. Even so, it cannot remain forever strong in a climate where the very emphasis on race, on blackness, as well as the radical resistance to white supremacy that fostered its inception, is deemed unimportant, no longer essential. Nor is it enough that it be a haven for a few individual scholars. It must enrich and expand the educational experience—the intellectual possibilities—of the Yale community, affirming in this effort the particular presence and work of black people.

In many ways the strength and weakness of African-American Studies reflects our collective condition as black people at Yale. If the program suffers, and I believe it does, from a crisis in valuation and engagement that leads to frustration, demoralization, alienation and despair—we all suffer that crisis. We are frustrated, demoralized, alienated, despairing. These feelings are expressed by black staff, students, and faculty. When black students feel that we as black professors have contempt for them, suspect their motives, refuse them affirmation—we are in crisis. When black professors feel that black students do not strive for excellence in our classes, try to get over, judge us harshly, exploit our concern—we are in crisis. When black professors are unable to engage in critical dialogue, denigrate and devalue one another's presence and work—we are in crisis. Our crisis is not unique. It is a reflection of black experience in all aspects of contemporary life. Our willingness to address this crisis affirms our link with the masses of black people striving to cope with the changing reality of black experience.

Significantly, this crisis in valuation is rooted in unresolved questions of identity and allegiance. In the 1960s and 1970s, universities appeared to embrace diversity as the fulfillment of an ideal circumstance for learning. There seemed to be a willingness to allow coexistence of similarity and difference. Blackness expressed through diversity of speech, dress, concerns, etc., could coexist with academic study and social life not informed by a black perspective. To celebrate difference was to react against conformity to a white, privileged class norm. It was a radical and subversive stance, with the potential to transform the entire educational process. Not only were many black students able to feel that we belonged at universities predominately peopled by white folks; we were eager to succeed and many of us did. Our commitment to transforming the lives of black people, to "racial uplift," to ending racial domination, was perfectly compatible with studying particular disciplines. This was important experiential enactment of education as the practice of freedom. In conversation with white historian Eugene Genovese, he fondly recalled those days at Yale in 1968 when black students met to discuss his lectures so that they might better challenge and critique, engaging in the mutual process of learning that is the very essence of liberatory pedagogy.

Contrast this with black students at Yale today raising the questions: "Does blackness exist?" and "Is there a black culture?" Uncertain about the value of racial solidarity, today's black students have been encouraged to believe that assimilation (to make similar, to be absorbed) is the way to succeed. They rarely critique the insistence of conformity to a white, privileged class norm but rather work to adapt this model of being. In contrast to the more radical model which seeks to transform the very definition of being, integrating a new model where difference is valued, adaptation is the goal. It is a passive rather than an active model. In *Education for Critical Consciousness*, Freire asserts:

> Integration with one's context, as distinguished from adaptation, is a distinctly human activity. Integration results from the capacity to adapt oneself to reality plus the critical capacity to make choices and transform that reality. To the extent that man loses his ability to make choices and is subjected to the choices of others, to the extent that his decisions are no longer his own because they result from external prescriptions, he is no longer integrated...
>
> The integrated person is person as Subject. In contrast, the adaptive person is person as object, adaptation representing at most a weak form of self defense. If man is incapable of changing reality, he adjusts himself instead. Adaptation is behavior characteristic of the animal sphere; exhibited by man, it is symptomatic of his dehumanization.

While assimilation is seen as an approach that ensures the successful entry of black people into the mainstream, at its very core it is dehumanizing. Embedded in the logic of assimilation is the white-supremacist assumption that blackness must be eradicated so that a new self, in this case a "white" self, can come into being. Of course, since we who are black can never be white, this very effort promotes and fosters serious psychological stress and even severe mental illness. My concern about the process of assimilation has deepened as I hear black students express pain and hurt, as I observe them suffer in ways that not only inhibit their ability to perform academically, but threaten their very existence. When I told a black female student the subject of my talk, her response was, "Why talk about freedom—why not just talk about sanity? We're trying to stay sane." Hearing students express pain and confusion has heightened my recognition that we are in crisis. It is especially troubling to hear black students confess that they are overwhelmed at times by feelings of alienation and despair, that they feel a loss of any sense of identity and meaning. Their despair echoes sentiments expressed by black people in circumstances where there is no choice, no option for change. Much of this pain is evoked by the effort to assimilate, which is a demand for self-negation.

Students who strive to assimilate while covertly trying to remain engaged with black experience suffer extreme frustration and psychological distress. In some circumstances, they may feel it is necessary to act as though racism does not exist, that their identity as a black person is not important. In other circumstances, they may deem it important to resist racism, to identify with black experience. Maintaining this separation is difficult, especially when these two contradictory longings converge and clash. Witness the black student hanging out with his white friends in downtown New Haven, on Chapel Street. A group of young black teenagers walks by, playing music, talking loud. One of his white peers turns to him and says in a matter-of-fact tone of voice, "Look at those niggers. They should be taken off the street and exterminated." Now that part of him that acknowledges blackness is shocked by the racism, deeply hurt by the recognition that caring and sharing in friendship has not altered this racial hatred. The assimilated part of him notices that the comment was made as though he were not black but just like his white peers, one with them in a fellowship of the chosen and superior, a gesture of inclusion in "whiteness" affirming that he has successfully assimilated. It is this part that says nothing—that silences the outrage, hurt, and anger he feels—that suppresses. On the surface, it may appear that he has coped with this situation, that he is fine, yet his psychological burden has intensified, the pain, confusion, and sense of betrayal a breeding ground for serious mental disturbance. The examples are endless, some less extreme, yet incidents like this one happen daily in classrooms, dormitories, on the street.

Without organized black liberation movement providing a framework for affirmation, for education for critical consciousness, concerned black students look to black professors for an example of ways to be whole, of ways to exist in this social context that allow celebration and acceptance of difference, ways to integrate rather than adapt, ways to be subject rather than object. More often than not they find similar fragmentation and confusion mirrored there, a more sophisticated version of assimilation: black professors who act as though they believe all black students are lazy and irresponsible; black professors who address questions and comments in classroom settings solely to white students; black professors who make an effort not to acknowledge in any way black students so as not to be open to the critique that they have preferences, a stance which may lead them to overcompensate by being overly attentive to non-black students. Perhaps we fear those white students who ask (as I have been asked): "If you like blackness and black students so much, why do you teach at Yale?" Or we fear being labelled racist. Given the white-supremacist context, it is difficult for students to understand that caring for the needs of one group does not negate caring for another group when what they have been taught is just the opposite.

Black students need to be acknowledged and affirmed by black professors. These gestures assure them that they should be studying at Yale, that they can succeed, that such success does not mean racial isolation. Absence of this recognition and affirmation promotes self doubt, reinforces the notion that assimilation is the only way to succeed. And of course a significant number of black students arrive at Yale already working to assimilate. While they may feel disturbed or even threatened by affirmation from black people, to ignore them further divides and separates us. Many black students want to have meaningful contact with black professors both in the classroom and outside it. Witness a black student coming to talk with a senior black professor about her desire to study an aspect of African-American women's history. He responds by stressing the paucity of available material, the difficulty of such research. Changing the subject, he wants to know her other interests and she tells him she wants to know more about China. Finally, he seems to notice her as if for the first time, and encourages her to pursue this subject. She comes away discouraged, confused, feeling devalued, wondering why he has not affirmed her desire to do scholarship on black women, especially since his scholarship focusses on black people.

Often it is easy for us as black professors to lose sight of the extent to which black students feel vulnerable, especially if such feelings are cloaked behind a mask of toughness and hard talk. This failure of insight is fostered as well, at institutions like Yale, where there is such strong emphasis on hierarchy, rank as that which not only identifies but separates and divides people. Definite assumptions about social behavior between those deemed in authority and those seen as subordinate inform relations between faculty and students. Given this context, it is easy to exercise power in a manner that wounds and diminishes, that reinforces domination.

Black faculty are influenced by this social context. Efforts individual professors make to humanize the teacher/student relationship may be perceived by colleagues as threatening the maintenance of hierarchical status. Some black professors believe a clear separation reinforced by behavior must be maintained between teacher and student (as in "students must know their place"); the origins of this metaphor are in our history. Such assumptions are based on the very notions of inferior and superior that inform white supremacy. To embrace them is to ally oneself with forces that reinforce and perpetuate domination. Understanding the harm and abuse we as black people can do to one another when we passively absorb and uncritically support notions of hierarchy, and working to construct alternative behavior strengthens our compassion and deepens our care for one another.

Internalized racism as expressed in our interactions with one another promotes divisiveness and fear. It is expressed in student/faculty encounters and in our encounters as professors with one another. Witness a new professor coming into an environment where there are few black women. She meets another black professor in her department who, when asked about his interests, says in an offhand manner, "I'm not into that Afro-American shit." Disassociating himself from blackness, he assumes an attitude of superiority, as though he has more accurately understood the way to succeed—assimilation, negation of the black self.

Then there are those black professors whose scholarship focusses on an aspect of black experience, to whom blackness is raw material for the production of a commodity with no relation to their social behavior. They may like studying and writing about black folks but would rather not associate with us. Reification and commodification of blackness make this possible. It leads to estrangement and alienation. Desiring to establish distance from one another, some black professors harshly criticize colleagues so as to ensure that they will not be seen as bonded, as connected. Such critiques may take the form of fierce denigration of one another's work, or even more serious acts of betrayal. Witness one black female professor engaging in a long discussion about another's class, emphasizing that she does not approve of the other's teaching methodology, denouncing it as illegitimate, anti-academic. Yet she has never participated in the other professor's class, heard her give a lecture, or talked with her about pedagogy. All her criticisms are based on hearsay. Such criticism not only creates unnecessary tension and hostility, it makes dialogue and constructive critique impossible. Recognizing the commonness of our experience as black faculty should serve as a basis for solidarity, promoting a willingness to challenge and confront one another so as to strengthen the collective community of scholars. If we can engage in meaningful critical discourse with one another, we enhance the likelihood that we can do so with our colleagues, with students.

African-American Studies should provide a context for critical engagement, especially among faculty. The presence of white professors in the program is occasionally cited by students as an indication that there is not real concern with affirmation of blackness. Yet if we make education into the practice of freedom, no committed, aware scholar can be excluded (this complaint is also made when there are large numbers of non-black students in African-American Studies courses). In theory, white professors involved with African-American Studies should be important allies, who understand white supremacy, who are committed to teaching in a manner that reflects this concern. If this is not so, then it is our responsibility individually and collectively to challenge, to educate for critical consciousness. To simply engage in denouncing that person to others represents failure to address this concern in a meaningful way. If African-American Studies programs at Yale and elsewhere are peopled by white professors who act in a manner that reinforces racial domination, the purpose of such programs is undermined and tragically perverted. Since we live historically (as individuals who change and are changed by events and circumstances), we have the power to transform reality, if we choose to act. Simply naming and identifying a problem does not solve it; naming is only one stage in the process of transformation. It is the courage to live our lives consciously and to act that will enable us to implement new strategies and goals. As an ethnically diverse group in African-American Studies, we should be a vanguard calling attention to the need for awareness of the politics of race; we should be continually engaged in a process of critical reflection. While our focus should not be exclusion, the emphasis must be on aware participation.

My teaching is sometimes criticized by non-black students, mostly whites, who complain that I show greater attention to black students; opposite criticism is made by black students. Affirmation of blackness does not necessitate inverting structures of domination nor does it imply devaluation of other experiences. Blackness is affirmed when students who have previously held narrow perceptions of black experience expand their consciousness; this is true for both non-black and black students. Significantly, we must focus on a policy of inclusion so as not to mirror oppressive structures, which does not mean that we do not engage in constructive critique and confrontation, or that we lose sight of the imperative of affirming blackness. Diversity is challenging precisely because it requires that we shift old paradigms, allowing for complexity.

These are only a few examples of situations and circumstances that reflect our crisis as black people at Yale. Acknowledgement is one significant way to begin the process of confrontation and transformation, of coming together. It is not an occasion for despair. Identifying ways we participate in the perpetuation of white supremacy, of racist domination expands our potential for intervention and transformation. Coming together to talk with one another is an important act of resistance, a gesture that shows our interest and concern. It enables us to see that we are a collective, that we can be a community of resistance. Together we can clarify our understanding of black experience, of similarity and difference as they determine our social relations, while sharing ways we remain self-affirming and whole as we do our scholarly work. Sharing personal strategies for negotiating this structure is a useful process of intervention. The more familiar we are, the more we communicate with one another, the greater our awareness that we are not isolated, the more we project our concerns in such a way that they impact on the experience of everyone here at Yale.

African-American Studies and the Afro-American Cultural Center are the primary places to make contact, to learn about courses and lectures that address particular aspects of black experience. How we value these settings will determine their current direction and their future. Now is a time to strengthen and intensify our engagement, renewing the spirit of unity and connection that enabled them to come into being. This is the true meaning of solidarity: that we consciously promote awareness of the politics of race, that we resist racism, that we define common concerns and interests we share as black people, that we recognize that fulfillment of this goal need not prevent us in any way from participating fully in the Yale community. Grounded in an affirmative sense of ourselves, of blackness, one that gives value and meaning to our experience, we bring an integrity of being to all other relations, educational and social, expanding, enriching these interactions.

When we commit ourselves to education as the practice of freedom, we participate in the making of an academic community where we can be and become intellectuals in the fullest and deepest sense of the word. We participate in a way of learning and being that makes the world more rather than less real, one that enables us to live life fully and freely. This is the joy in our quest.

11

keeping close to home: class and education

We are both awake in the almost dark of 5 a.m. Everyone else is sound asleep. Mama asks the usual questions. Telling me to look around, make sure I have everything, scolding me because I am uncertain about the actual time the bus arrives. By 5:30 we are waiting outside the closed station. Alone together, we have a chance to really talk. Mama begins. Angry with her children, especially the ones who whisper behind her back, she says bitterly, "Your childhood could not have been that bad. You were fed and clothed. You did not have to do without—that's more than a lot of folks have and I just can't stand the way y'all go on." The hurt in her voice saddens me. I have always wanted to protect mama from hurt, to ease her burdens. Now I am part of what troubles. Confronting me, she says accusingly, "It's not just the other children. You talk too much about the past. You don't just listen." And I do talk. Worse, I write about it.

Mama has always come to each of her children seeking different responses. With me she expresses the disappointment, hurt, and anger of betrayal: anger that her children are so critical, that we can't even have the sense to like the presents she sends. She says, "From now on there will be no presents. I'll just stick some money in a little envelope the way the rest of you do. Nobody wants criticism. Everybody can criticize me but I am supposed to say nothing." When I try to talk, my voice sounds like a twelve year old. When I try to talk, she speaks louder, interrupting me, even though

73

she has said repeatedly, "Explain it to me, this talk about the past." I struggle to return to my thirty-five year old self so that she will know by the
sound of my voice that we are two women talking together. It is only when
I state firmly in my very adult voice, "Mama, you are not listening," that
she becomes quiet. She waits. Now that I have her attention, I fear that my
explanations will be lame, inadequate. "Mama," I begin, "people usually
go to therapy because they feel hurt inside, because they have pain that
will not stop, like a wound that continually breaks open, that does not
heal. And often these hurts, that pain has to do with things that have happened in the past, sometimes in childhood, often in childhood, or things
that we believe happened." She wants to know, "What hurts, what hurts
are you talking about?" "Mom, I can't answer that. I can't speak for all of
us, the hurts are different for everybody. But the point is you try to make
the hurt better, to heal it, by understanding how it came to be. And I know
you feel mad when we say something happened or hurt that you don't
remember being that way, but the past isn't like that, we don't have the
same memory of it. We remember things differently. You know that. And
sometimes folk feel hurt about stuff and you just don't know or didn't realize it, and they need to talk about it. Surely you understand the need to
talk about it."

Our conversation is interrupted by the sight of my uncle walking
across the park toward us. We stop to watch him. He is on his way to work
dressed in a familiar blue suit. They look alike, these two who rarely discuss the past. This interruption makes me think about life in a small town.
You always see someone you know. Interruptions, intrusions are part of
daily life. Privacy is difficult to maintain. We leave our private space in the
car to greet him. After the hug and kiss he has given me every year since
I was born, they talk about the day's funerals. In the distance the bus approaches. He walks away knowing that they will see each other later. Just
before I board the bus I turn, staring into my mother's face. I am momen-
tarily back in time, seeing myself eighteen years ago, at this same bus stop,
staring into my mother's face, continually turning back, waving farewell as
I returned to college—that experience which first took me away from our
town, from family. Departing was as painful then as it is now. Each movement away makes return harder. Each separation intensifies distance, both
physical and emotional.

To a southern black girl from a working-class background who had
never been on a city bus, who had never stepped on an escalator, who
had never travelled by plane, leaving the comfortable confines of a small
town Kentucky life to attend Stanford University was not just frightening;
it was utterly painful. My parents had not been delighted that I had been
accepted and adamantly opposed my going so far from home. At the time,
I did not see their opposition as an expression of their fear that they would
lose me forever. Like many working-class folks, they feared what college
education might do to their children's minds even as they unenthusiasti-

cally acknowledged its importance. They did not understand why I could not attend a college nearby, an all-black college. To them, any college would do. I would graduate, become a school teacher, make a decent living and a good marriage. And even though they reluctantly and skeptically supported my educational endeavors, they also subjected them to constant harsh and bitter critique. It is difficult for me to talk about my parents and their impact on me because they have always felt wary, ambivalent, mistrusting of my intellectual aspirations even as they have been caring and supportive. I want to speak about these contradictions because sorting through them, seeking resolution and reconciliation has been important to me both as it affects my development as a writer, my effort to be fully self-realized, and my longing to remain close to the family and community that provided the groundwork for much of my thinking, writing, and being.

Studying at Stanford, I began to think seriously about class differences. To be materially underprivileged at a university where most folks (with the exception of workers) are materially privileged provokes such thought. Class differences were boundaries no one wanted to face or talk about. It was easier to downplay them, to act as though we were all from privileged backgrounds, to work around them, to confront them privately in the solitude of one's room, or to pretend that just being chosen to study at such an institution meant that those of us who did not come from privilege were already in transition toward privilege. To not long for such transition marked one as rebellious, as unlikely to succeed. It was a kind of treason not to believe that it was better to be identified with the world of material privilege than with the world of the working class, the poor. No wonder our working-class parents from poor backgrounds feared our entry into such a world, intuiting perhaps that we might learn to be ashamed of where we had come from, that we might never return home, or come back only to lord it over them.

Though I hung with students who were supposedly radical and chic, we did not discuss class. I talked to no one about the sources of my shame, how it hurt me to witness the contempt shown the brown-skinned Filipina maids who cleaned our rooms, or later my concern about the $100 a month I paid for a room off-campus which was more than half of what my parents paid for rent. I talked to no one about my efforts to save money, to send a little something home. Yet these class realities separated me from fellow students. We were moving in different directions. I did not intend to forget my class background or alter my class allegiance. And even though I received an education designed to provide me with a bourgeois sensibility, passive acquiescence was not my only option. I knew that I could resist. I could rebel. I could shape the direction and focus of the various forms of knowledge available to me. Even though I sometimes envied and longed for greater material advantages (particularly at vacation times when I would be one of few if any students remaining in the dormitory because there was no money for travel), I did not share the sensibility and values of my peers. That was important—class was not just about money; it was about values which showed and determined behavior. While I often needed more money, I never needed a new set of beliefs and values. For example, I was profoundly shocked and disturbed when peers would talk about their parents without respect, or would even say that they hated their parents. This was especially troubling to me when it seemed that these parents were caring and concerned. It was often explained to me that such hatred was "healthy and normal." To my white, middle-class California roommate, I explained the way we were taught to value our parents and their care, to understand that they were not obligated to give us care. She would always shake her head, laughing all the while, and say, "Missy, you will learn that it's different here, that we think differently." She was right. Soon, I lived alone, like the one Mormon student who kept to himself as he made a concentrated effort to remain true to his religious beliefs and values. Later in graduate school I found that classmates believed "lower class" people had no beliefs and values. I was silent in such discussions, disgusted by their ignorance.

Carol Stack's anthropological study, *All Our Kin,* was one of the first books I read which confirmed my experiential understanding that within black culture (especially among the working class and poor, particularly in southern states), a value system emerged that was counter-hegemonic, that challenged notions of individualism and private property so important to the maintenance of white-supremacist, capitalist patriarchy. Black folk created in marginal spaces a world of community and collectivity where resources were shared. In the preface to *Feminist Theory: from margin to center,* I talked about how the point of difference, this marginality can be the space for the formation of an oppositional world view. That world view must be articulated, named if it is to provide a sustained blueprint for change. Unfortunately, there has existed no consistent framework for such naming. Consequently both the experience of this difference and documentation of it (when it occurs) gradually loses presence and meaning.

Much of what Stack documented about the "culture of poverty," for example, would not describe interactions among most black poor today irrespective of geographical setting. Since the black people she described did not acknowledge (if they recognized it in theoretical terms) the oppositional value of their world view, apparently seeing it more as a survival strategy determined less by conscious efforts to oppose oppressive race and class biases than by circumstance, they did not attempt to establish a framework to transmit their beliefs and values from generation to generation. When circumstances changed, values altered. Efforts to assimilate the values and beliefs of privileged white people, presented through media like television, undermine and destroy potential structures of opposition.

Increasingly, young black people are encouraged by the dominant culture (and by those black people who internalize the values of this hegemony) to believe that assimilation is the only possible way to survive, to succeed. Without the framework of an organized civil rights or black resistance struggle, individual and collective efforts at black liberation that focus on the primacy of self-definition and self-determination often go unrecognized. It is crucial that those among us who resist and rebel, who survive and succeed, speak openly and honestly about our lives and the nature of our personal struggles, the means by which we resolve and reconcile contradictions. This is no easy task. Within the educational institutions where we learn to develop and strengthen our writing and analytical skills, we also learn to think, write, and talk in a manner that shifts attention away from personal experience. Yet if we are to reach our people and all people, if we are to remain connected (especially those of us whose familial backgrounds are poor and working-class), we must understand that the telling of one's personal story provides a meaningful example, a way for folks to identify and connect.

Combining personal with critical analysis and theoretical perspectives can engage listeners who might other wise feel estranged, alienated. To speak simply with language that is accessible to as many folks as possible is also important. Speaking about one's personal experience or speaking with simple language is often considered by academics and/or intellectuals (irrespective of their political inclinations) to be a sign of intellectual weakness or even anti-intellectualism. Lately, when I speak, I do not stand in place—reading my paper, making little or no eye contact with audiences—but instead make eye contact, talk extemporaneously, digress, and address the audience directly. I have been told that people assume I am not prepared, that I am anti-intellectual, unprofessional (a concept that has everything to do with class as it determines actions and behavior), or that I am reinforcing the stereotype of black people as non-theoretical and gutsy.

Such criticism was raised recently by fellow feminist scholars after a talk I gave at Northwestern University at a conference on "Gender, Culture, Politics" to an audience that was mainly students and academics. I deliberately chose to speak in a very basic way, thinking especially about the few community folks who had come to hear me. Weeks later, Kum-Kum Sangari, a fellow participant who shared with me what was said when I was no longer present, and I engaged in quite rigorous critical dialogue about the way my presentation had been perceived primarily by privileged white female academics. She was concerned that I not mask my knowledge of theory, that I not appear anti-intellectual. Her critique compelled me to articulate concerns that I am often silent about with colleagues. I spoke about class allegiance and revolutionary commitments, explaining that it was disturbing to me that intellectual radicals who speak about transforming society, ending the domination of race, sex, class, cannot break with behavior patterns that reinforce and perpetuate domination, or continue to use as their sole reference point how we might be or are perceived by those who dominate, whether or not we gain their acceptance and approval.

This is a primary contradiction which raises the issue of whether or not the academic setting is a place where one can be truly radical or subversive. Concurrently, the use of a language and style of presentation that alienates most folks who are not also academically trained reinforces the notion that the academic world is separate from real life, that everyday world where we constantly adjust our language and behavior to meet diverse needs. The academic setting is separate only when we work to make it so. It is a false dichotomy which suggests that academics and/or intellectuals can only speak to one another, that we cannot hope to speak with the masses. What is true is that we make choices, that we choose our audiences, that we choose voices to hear and voices to silence. If I do not speak in a language that can be understood, then there is little chance for dialogue. This issue of language and behavior is a central contradiction all radical intellectuals, particularly those who are members of oppressed groups, must continually confront and work to resolve. One of the clear and present dangers that exists when we move outside our class of origin, our collective ethnic experience, and enter hierarchical institutions which daily reinforce domination by race, sex, and class, is that we gradually assume a mindset similar to those who dominate and oppress, that we lose critical consciousness because it is not reinforced or affirmed by the environment. We must be ever vigilant. It is important that we know who we are speaking to, who we most want to hear us, who we most long to move, motivate, and touch with our words.

When I first came to New Haven to teach at Yale, I was truly surprised by the marked class divisions between black folks—students and professors—who identify with Yale and those black folks who work at Yale or in surrounding communities. Style of dress and self-presentation are most often the central markers of one's position. I soon learned that the black folks who spoke on the street were likely to be part of the black community and those who carefully shifted their glance were likely to be associated with Yale. Walking with a black female colleague one day, I spoke to practically every black person in sight (a gesture which reflects my upbringing), an action which disturbed my companion. Since I addressed black folk who were clearly not associated with Yale, she wanted to know whether or not I knew them. That was funny to me. "Of course not," I answered. Yet when I thought about it seriously, I realized that in a deep way, I knew them for they, and not my companion or most of my colleagues at Yale, resemble my family. Later that year, in a black women's support group I started for undergraduates, students from poor backgrounds spoke about the shame they sometimes feel when faced with the reality of their connection to working-class and poor black people. One student confessed that her father is a street person, addicted to drugs, someone who begs from passersby. She, like other Yale students, turns away from street people often, sometimes showing anger or contempt; she hasn't wanted anyone to know that she was related to this kind of person. She struggles with this, wanting to find a way to acknowledge and affirm this reality, to claim this connection. The group asked me and one another what we do to remain connected, to honor the bonds we have with working-class and poor people even as our class experience alters.

Maintaining connections with family and community across class boundaries demands more than just summary recall of where one's roots are, where one comes from. It requires knowing, naming, and being ever-mindful of those aspects of one's past that have enabled and do enable one's self-development in the present, that sustain and support, that enrich. One must also honestly confront barriers that do exist, aspects of that past that do diminish. My parent's ambivalence about my love for reading led to intense conflict. They (especially my mother) would work to ensure that I had access to books, but would threaten to burn the books or throw them away if I did not conform to other expectations. Or they would insist that reading too much would drive me insane. Their ambivalence nurtured in me a like uncertainty about the value and significance of intellectual endeavor which took years for me to unlearn. While this aspect of our class reality was one that wounded and diminished, their vigilant insistence that being smart did not make me a "better" or "superior" person (which often got on my nerves because I think I wanted to have that sense that it did indeed set me apart, make me better) made a profound impression. From them I learned to value and respect various skills and talents folk might have, not just to value people who read books and talk about ideas. They and my grandparents might say about somebody, "Now he don't read nor write a lick, but he can tell a story," or as my grandmother would say, "call out the hell in words."

Empty romanticization of poor or working-class backgrounds undermines the possibility of true connection. Such connection is based on understanding difference in experience and perspective and working to mediate and negotiate these terrains. Language is a crucial issue for folk whose movement outside the boundaries of poor and working-class backgrounds changes the nature and direction of their speech. Coming to Stanford with my own version of a Kentucky accent, which I think of always as a strong sound quite different from Tennessee or Georgia speech, I learned to speak differently while maintaining the speech of my region, the sound of my family and community. This was of course much easier to keep up when I returned home to stay often. In recent years, I have endeavored to use various speaking styles in the classroom as a teacher and find it disconcerts those who feel that the use of a particular patois excludes them as listeners, even if there is translation into the usual, acceptable mode of speech. Learning to listen to different voices, hearing different speech challenges the notion that we must all assimilate—share a single, similar talk—in educational institutions. Language reflects the culture from which we emerge. To deny ourselves daily use of speech patterns that are common and familiar, that embody the unique and distinctive aspect of our self is one of the ways we become estranged and alienated from our past. It is important for us to have as many languages on hand as we can know or learn. It is important for those of us who are black, who speak in particular patois as well as standard English to express ourselves in both ways.

Often I tell students from poor and working-class backgrounds that if you believe what you have learned and are learning in schools and universities separates you from your past, this is precisely what will happen. It is important to stand firm in the conviction that nothing can truly separate us from our pasts when we nurture and cherish that connection. An important strategy for maintaining contact is ongoing acknowledgement of the primacy of one's past, of one's background, affirming the reality that such bonds are not severed automatically solely because one enters a new environment or moves toward a different class experience.

Again, I do not wish to romanticize this effort, to dismiss the reality of conflict and contradiction. During my time at Stanford, I did go through a period of more than a year when I did not return home. That period was one where I felt that it was simply too difficult to mesh my profoundly disparate realities. Critical reflection about the choice I was making, particularly about why I felt a choice had to be made, pulled me through this difficult time. Luckily I recognized that the insistence on choosing between the world of family and community and the new world of privileged white people and privileged ways of knowing was imposed upon me by the outside. It is as though a mythical contract had been signed somewhere which demanded of us black folks that once we entered these spheres we would immediately give up all vestiges of our underprivileged past. It was my responsibility to formulate a way of being that would allow me to participate fully in my new environment while integrating and maintaining aspects of the old.

One of the most tragic manifestations of the pressure black people feel to assimilate is expressed in the internalization of racist perspectives. I was shocked and saddened when I first heard black professors at Stanford downgrade and express contempt for black students, expecting us to do poorly, refusing to establish nurturing bonds. At every university I have attended as a student or worked at as a teacher, I have heard similar attitudes expressed with little or no understanding of factors that might prevent brilliant black students from performing to their full capability. Within universities, there are few educational and social spaces where students who wish to affirm positive ties to ethnicity—to blackness, to working-class backgrounds—can receive affirmation and support. Ideologically, the message is clear—assimilation is the way to gain acceptance and approval from those in power.

Many white people enthusiastically supported Richard Rodriguez's vehement contention in his autobiography, *Hunger of Memory*, that attempts to maintain ties with his Chicano background impeded his progress, that he had to sever ties with community and kin to succeed at Stanford and in the larger world, that family language, in his case Spanish, had to be made secondary or discarded. If the terms of success as defined by the standards of ruling groups within white-supremacist, capitalist patriarchy are the only standards that exist, then assimilation is indeed necessary. But they are not. Even in the face of powerful structures of domination, it remains possible for each of us, especially those of us who are members of oppressed and/or exploited groups as well as those radical visionaries who may have race, class, and sex privilege, to define and determine alternative standards, to decide on the nature and extent of compromise. Standards by which one's success is measured, whether student or professor, are quite different for those of us who wish to resist reinforcing the domination of race, sex, and class, who work to maintain and strengthen our ties with the oppressed, with those who lack material privilege, with our families who are poor and working-class.

When I wrote my first book, *Ain't I A Woman: black women and feminism*, the issue of class and its relationship to who one's reading audience might be came up for me around my decision not to use footnotes, for which I have been sharply criticized. I told people that my concern was that footnotes set class boundaries for readers, determining who a book is for. I was shocked that many academic folks scoffed at this idea. I shared that I went into working-class black communities as well as talked with family and friends to survey whether or not they ever read books with footnotes and found that they did not. A few did not know what they were, but most folks saw them as indicating that a book was for college-educated people. These responses influenced my decision. When some of my more radical, college-educated friends freaked out about the absence of footnotes, I seriously questioned how we could ever imagine revolutionary transformation of society if such a small shift in direction could be viewed as threatening. Of course, many folks warned that the absence of footnotes would make the work less credible in academic circles. This information also highlighted the way in which class informs our choices. Certainly I did feel that choosing to use simple language, absence of footnotes, etc. would mean I was jeopardizing the possibility of being taken seriously in academic circles but then this was a political matter and a political decision. It utterly delights me that this has proven not to be the case and that the book is read by many academics as well as by people who are not college-educated.

Always our first response when we are motivated to conform or compromise within structures that reinforce domination must be to engage in critical reflection. Only by challenging ourselves to push against oppressive boundaries do we make the radical alternative possible, expanding the realm and scope of critical inquiry. Unless we share radical strategies, ways of rethinking and revisioning with students, with kin and community, with a larger audience, we risk perpetuating the stereotype that we succeed because we are the exception, different from the rest of our people. Since I left home and entered college, I am often asked, usually by white people, if my sisters and brothers are also high achievers. At the root of this question is the longing for reinforcement of the belief in "the exception" which enables race, sex, and class biases to remain intact. I am careful to separate what it means to be exceptional from a notion of "the exception."

Frequently I hear smart black folks, from poor and working-class backgrounds, stressing their frustration that at times family and community do not recognize that they are exceptional. Absence of positive affirmation clearly diminishes the longing to excel in academic endeavors. Yet it is important to distinguish between the absence of basic positive affirmation and the longing for continued reinforcement that we are special. Usually liberal white folks will willingly offer continual reinforcement of us as exceptions—as special. This can be both patronizing and very seductive. Since we often work in situations where we are isolated from other black folks, we can easily begin to feel that encouragement from white people is the primary or only source of support and recognition. Given the internalization of racism, it is easy to view this support as more validating and legitimizing than similar support from black people. Still, nothing takes the place of being valued and appreciated by one's own, by one's family and community. We share a mutual and reciprocal responsibility for affirming one another's successes. Sometimes we have to talk to our folks about the fact that we need their ongoing support and affirmation, that it is unique and special to us. In some cases we may never receive desired recognition and acknowledgement of specific achievements from kin. Rather than seeing this as a basis for estrangement, for severing connection, it is useful to explore other sources of nourishment and support.

I do not know that my mother's mother ever acknowledged my college education except to ask me once, "How can you live so far away from your people?" Yet she gave me sources of affirmation and nourishment, sharing the legacy of her quilt-making, of family history, of her incredible way with words. Recently, when our father retired after more than thirty years of work as a janitor, I wanted to pay tribute to this experience, to identify links between his work and my own as writer and teacher. Reflecting on our family past, I recalled ways he had been an impressive example of diligence and hard work, approaching tasks with a seriousness of concentration I work to mirror and develop, with a discipline I struggle to maintain. Sharing these thoughts with him keeps us connected, nurtures our respect for each other, maintaining a space, however large or small, where we can talk.

Open, honest communication is the most important way we maintain relationships with kin and community as our class experience and backgrounds change. It is as vital as the sharing of resources. Often financial assistance is given in circumstances where there is no meaningful contact. However helpful, this can also be an expression of estrangement and alienation. Communication between black folks from various experiences of material privilege was much easier when we were all in segregated communities sharing common experiences in relation to social institutions. Without this grounding, we must work to maintain ties, connection. We must assume greater responsibility for making and maintaining contact, connections that can shape our intellectual visions and inform our radical commitments.

The most powerful resource any of us can have as we study and teach in university settings is full understanding and appreciation of the richness, beauty, and primacy of our familial and community backgrounds. Maintaining awareness of class differences, nurturing ties with the poor and working-class people who are our most intimate kin, our comrades in struggle, transforms and enriches our intellectual experience. Education as the practice of freedom becomes not a force which fragments or separates, but one that brings us closer, expanding our definitions of home and community.

12

violence in intimate relationships:
a feminist perspective

We were on the freeway, going home from San Francisco. He was driving. We were arguing. He had told me repeatedly to shut up. I kept talking. He took his hand from the steering wheel and threw it back, hitting my mouth—my open mouth, blood gushed, and I felt an intense pain. I was no longer able to say any words, only to make whimpering, sobbing sounds as the blood dripped on my hands, on the handkerchief I held too tightly. He did not stop the car. He drove home. I watched him pack his suitcase. It was a holiday. He was going away to have fun. When he left I washed my mouth. My jaw was swollen and it was difficult for me to open it.

I called the dentist the next day and made an appointment. When the female voice asked what I needed to see the doctor about, I told her I had been hit in the mouth. Conscious of race, sex, and class issues, I wondered how I would be treated in this white doctor's office. My face was no longer swollen so there was nothing to identify me as a woman who had been hit, as a black woman with a bruised and swollen jaw. When the dentist asked me what had happened to my mouth, I described it calmly and succinctly. He made little jokes about, "How we can't have someone doing this to us now, can we?" I said nothing. The damage was repaired. Through it all, he talked to me as if I were a child, someone he had to handle gingerly or otherwise I might become hysterical.

This is one way women who are hit by men and seek medical care are seen. People within patriarchal society imagine that women are hit because we are hysterical, because we are beyond reason. It is most often the person who is hitting that is beyond reason, who is hysterical, who has lost complete control over responses and actions.

Growing up, I had always thought that I would never allow any man to hit me and live. I would kill him. I had seen my father hit my mother once and I wanted to kill him. My mother said to me then, "You are too young to know, too young to understand." Being a mother in a culture that supports and promotes domination, a patriarchal, white-supremacist culture, she did not discuss how she felt or what she meant. Perhaps it would have been too difficult for her to speak about the confusion of being hit by someone you are intimate with, someone you love. In my case, I was hit by my companion at a time in life when a number of forces in the world outside our home had already "hit" me, so to speak, made me painfully aware of my powerlessness, my marginality. It seemed then that I was confronting being black and female and without money in the worst possible ways. My world was spinning. I had already lost a sense of grounding and security. The memory of this experience has stayed with me as I have grown as a feminist, as I have thought deeply and read much on male violence against women, on adult violence against children.

In this essay, I do not intend to concentrate attention solely on male physical abuse of females. It is crucial that feminists call attention to physical abuse in all its forms. In particular, I want to discuss being physically abused in singular incidents by someone you love. Few people who are hit once by someone they love respond in the way they might to a singular physical assault by a stranger. Many children raised in households where hitting has been a normal response by primary caretakers react ambivalently to physical assaults as adults, especially if they are being hit by someone who cares for them and whom they care for. Often female parents use physical abuse as a means of control. There is continued need for feminist research that examines such violence. Alice Miller has done insightful work on the impact of hitting even though she is at times anti-feminist in her perspective. (Often in her work, mothers are blamed, as if their responsibility in parenting is greater than that of fathers.) Feminist discussions of violence against women should be expanded to include a recognition of the ways in which women use abusive physical force toward children not only to challenge the assumptions that women are likely to be nonviolent, but also to add to our understanding of why children who were hit growing up are often hit as adults or hit others.

Recently, I began a conversation with a group of black adults about hitting children. They all agreed that hitting was sometimes necessary. A professional black male in a southern family setting with two children commented on the way he punished his daughters. Sitting them down, he would first interrogate them about the situation or circumstance for which they were being punished. He said with great pride, "I want them to be able to understand fully why they are being punished." I responded by saying that "they will likely become women whom a lover will attack using the same procedure you who have loved them so well used and they will not know how to respond." He resisted the idea that his behavior would have any impact on their responses to violence as adult women. I pointed to case after case of women in intimate relationships with men (and sometimes women) who are subjected to the same form of interrogation and punishment they experienced as children, who accept their lover assuming an abusive, authoritarian role. Children who are the victims of physical abuse—whether one beating or repeated beatings, one violent push or several—whose wounds are inflicted by a loved one, experience an extreme sense of dislocation. The world one has most intimately known, in which one felt relatively safe and secure, has collapsed. Another world has come into being, one filled with terrors, where it is difficult to distinguish between a safe situation and a dangerous one, a gesture of love and a violent, uncaring gesture. There is a feeling of vulnerability, exposure, that never goes away, that lurks beneath the surface. I know. I was one of those children. Adults hit by loved ones usually experience similar sensations of dislocation, of loss, of new found terrors.

Many children who are hit have never known what it feels like to be cared for, loved without physical aggression or abusive pain. Hitting is such a widespread practice that any of us are lucky if we can go through life without having this experience. One undiscussed aspect of the reality of children who are hit finding themselves as adults in similar circumstances is that we often share with friends and lovers the framework of our childhood pains and this may determine how they respond to us in difficult situations. We share the ways we are wounded and expose vulnerable areas. Often, these revelations provide a detailed model for anyone who wishes to wound or hurt us. While the literature about physical abuse often points to the fact that children who are abused are likely to become abusers or be abused, there is no attention given to sharing woundedness in such a way that we let intimate others know exactly what can be done to hurt us, to make us feel as though we are caught in the destructive patterns we have struggled to break. When partners create scenarios of abuse similar, if not exactly the same, to those we have experienced in childhood, the wounded person is hurt not only by the physical pain but by the feeling of calculated betrayal. Betrayal. When we are physically hurt by loved ones, we feel betrayed. We can no longer trust that care can be sustained. We are wounded, damaged—hurt to our hearts.

Feminist work calling attention to male violence against women has helped create a climate where the issues of physical abuse by loved ones can be freely addressed, especially sexual abuse within families. Exploration of male violence against women by feminists and non-feminists shows a connection between childhood experience of being hit by loved ones and the later occurrence of violence in adult relationships. While there is much material available discussing physical abuse of women by men, usually extreme physical abuse, there is not much discussion of the impact that one incident of hitting may have on a person in an intimate relationship, or how the person who is hit recovers from that experience. Increasingly, in discussion with women about physical abuse in relationships, irrespective of sexual preference, I find that most of us have had the experience of being violently hit at least once. There is little discussion of how we are damaged by such experiences (especially if we have been hit as children), of the ways we cope and recover from this wounding. This is an important area for feminist research precisely because many cases of extreme physical abuse begin with an isolated incident of hitting. Attention must be given to understanding and stopping these isolated incidents if we are to eliminate the possibility that women will be at risk in intimate relationships.

Critically thinking about issues of physical abuse has led me to question the way our culture, the way we as feminist advocates focus on the issue of violence and physical abuse by loved ones. The focus has been on male violence against women and, in particular, male sexual abuse of children. Given the nature of patriarchy, is has been necessary for feminists to focus on extreme cases to make people confront the issue, and acknowledge it to be serious and relevant. Unfortunately, an exclusive focus on extreme cases can and does lead us to ignore the more frequent, more common, yet less extreme case of occasional hitting. Women are also less likely to acknowledge occasional hitting for fear that they will then be seen as someone who is in a bad relationship or someone whose life is out of control. Currently, the literature about male violence against women identifies the physically abused woman as a "battered woman." While it has been important to have an accessible terminology to draw attention to the issue of male violence against women, the terms used reflect biases because they call attention to only one type of violence in intimate relationships. The term "battered woman" is problematical. It is not a term that emerged from feminist work on male violence against women; it was already used by psychologists and sociologists in the literature on domestic violence. This label "battered woman" places primary emphasis on physical assaults that are continuous, repeated, and unrelenting. The focus is on extreme violence, with little effort to link these cases with the everyday acceptance within intimate relationships of physical abuse that is not extreme, that may not be repeated. Yet these lesser forms of physical abuse damage individuals psychologically and, if not properly addressed and recovered from, can set the stage for more extreme incidents.

Most importantly, the term "battered woman" is used as though it constitutes a separate and unique category of womanness, as though it is an identity, a mark that sets one apart rather than being simply a descriptive term. It is as though the experience of being repeatedly violently hit is the sole defining characteristic of a woman's identity and all other aspects of who she is and what her experience has been are submerged. When I was hit, I too used the popular phrases "batterer," "battered woman," "battering" even though I did not feel that these words adequately described being hit once. However, these were the terms that people would listen to, would see as important, significant (as if it is not really significant for an individual, and more importantly for a woman, to be hit once). My partner was angry to be labelled a batterer by me. He was reluctant to talk about the experience of hitting me precisely because he did not want to be labelled a batterer. I had hit him once (not as badly as he had hit me) and I did not think of myself as a batterer. For both of us, these terms were inadequate. Rather than enabling us to cope effectively and positively with a negative situation, they were part of all the mechanisms of denial; they made us want to avoid confronting what had happened. This is the case for many people who are hit and those who hit.

Women who are hit once by men in their lives, and women who are hit repeatedly do not want to be placed in the category of "battered woman" because it is a label that appears to strip us of dignity, to deny that there has been any integrity in the relationships we are in. A person physically assaulted by a stranger or a casual friend with whom they are not intimate may be hit once or repeatedly but they do not have to be placed into a category before doctors, lawyers, family, counselors, etc. take their problem seriously. Again, it must be stated that establishing categories and terminology has been part of the effort to draw public attention to the seriousness of male violence against women in intimate relationships. Even though the use of convenient labels and categories has made it easier to identify problems of physical abuse, it does not mean the terminology should not be critiqued from a feminist perspective and changed if necessary.

Recently, I had an experience assisting a woman who had been brutally attacked by her husband (she never commented on whether this was the first incident or not), which caused me to reflect anew on the use of the term "battered woman." This young woman was not engaged in feminist thinking or aware that "battered woman" was a category. Her husband had tried to choke her to death. She managed to escape from him with only the clothes she was wearing. After she recovered from the trauma, she considered going back to this relationship. As a church-going woman, she believed that her marriage vows were sacred and that she should try to make the relationship work. In an effort to share my feeling that this could place her at great risk, I brought her Lenore Walker's *The Battered Woman* because it seemed to me that there was much that she was not revealing, that she felt alone, and that the experiences she would read about in the book would give her a sense that other women had experienced what she was going through. I hoped reading the book would give her the courage to confront the reality of her situation. Yet I found it difficult to share because I could see that her self-esteem had already been greatly attacked, that she had lost a sense of her worth and value, and that possibly this categorizing of her identity would add to the feeling that she should just forget, be silent (and certainly returning to a situation where one is likely to be abused is one way to mask the severity of the problem). Still I had to try. When I first gave her the book, it disappeared. An unidentified family member had thrown it away. They felt that she would be making a serious mistake if she began to see herself as an absolute victim which they felt the label "battered woman" implied. I stressed that she should ignore the labels and read the content. I believed the experience shared in this book helped give her the courage to be critical of her situation, to take constructive action.

Her response to the label "battered woman," as well as the responses of other women who have been victims of violence in intimate relationships, compelled me to critically explore further the use of this term. In conversation with many women, I found that it was seen as a stigmatizing label, one which victimized women seeking help felt themselves in no condition to critique. As in, "who cares what anybody is calling it—I just want to stop this pain." Within patriarchal society, women who are victimized by male violence have had to pay a price for breaking the silence and naming the problem. They have had to be seen as fallen women, who have failed in their "feminine" role to sensitize and civilize the beast in the man. A category like "battered woman" risks reinforcing this notion that the hurt woman, not only the rape victim, becomes a social pariah, set apart, marked forever by this experience.

A distinction must be made between having a terminology that enables women, and all victims of violent acts, to name the problem and categories of labeling that may inhibit that naming. When individuals are wounded, we are indeed often scarred, often damaged in ways that do set us apart from those who have not experienced a similar wounding, but an essential aspect of the recovery process is the healing of the wound, the removal of the scar. This is an empowering process that should not be diminished by labels that imply this wounding experience is the most significant aspect of identity.

As I have already stated, overemphasis on extreme cases of violent abuse may lead us to ignore the problem of occasional hitting, and it may make it difficult for women to talk about this problem. A critical issue that is not fully examined and written about in great detail by researchers who study and work with victims is the recovery process. There is a dearth of material discussing the recovery process of individuals who have been physically abused. In those cases where an individual is hit only once in an intimate relationship, however violently, there may be no recognition at all of the negative impact of this experience. There may be no conscious attempt by the victimized person to work at restoring her or his well-being, even if the person seeks therapeutic help, because the one incident may not be seen as serious or damaging. Alone and in isolation, the person who has been hit must struggle to regain broken trust—to forge some strategy of recovery. Individuals are often able to process an experience of being hit mentally that may not be processed emotionally. Many women I talked with felt that even after the incident was long forgotten, their bodies remain troubled. Instinctively, the person who has been hit may respond fearfully to any body movement on the part of a loved one that is similar to the posture used when pain was inflicted.

Being hit once by a partner can forever diminish sexual relationships if there has been no recovery process. Again there is little written about ways folks recover physically in their sexualities as loved ones who continue to be sexual with those who have hurt them. In most cases, sexual relationships are dramatically altered when hitting has occurred. The sexual realm may be the one space where the person who has been hit experiences again the sense of vulnerability, which may also arouse fear. This can lead either to an attempt to avoid sex or to unacknowledged sexual withdrawal wherein the person participates but is passive. I talked with women who had been hit by lovers who described sex as an ordeal, the one space where they confront their inability to trust a partner who has broken trust. One woman emphasized that to her, being hit was a "violation of her body space" and that she felt from then on she had to protect that space. This response, though a survival strategy, does not lead to healthy recovery.

Often, women who are hit in intimate relationships with male or female lovers feel as though we have lost an innocence that cannot be regained. Yet this very notion of innocence is connected to passive acceptance of concepts of romantic love under patriarchy which have served to mask problematic realities in relationships. The process of recovery must include a critique of this notion of innocence which is often linked to an unrealistic and fantastic vision of love and romance. It is only in letting go of the perfect, no-work, happily-ever-after union idea, that we can rid our psyches of the sense that we have failed in some way by not having such relationships. Those of us who never focussed on the negative impact of being hit as children find it necessary to reexamine the past in a therapeutic manner as part of our recovery process. Strategies that helped us survive as children may be detrimental for us to use in adult relationships.

Talking about being hit by loved ones with other women, both as children and as adults, I found that many of us had never really thought very much about our own relationship to violence. Many of us took pride in never feeling violent, never hitting. We had not thought deeply about our relationship to inflicting physical pain. Some of us expressed terror and awe when confronted with physical strength on the part of others. For us, the healing process included the need to learn how to use physical force constructively, to remove the terror—the dread. Despite the research that suggests children who are hit may become adults who hit—women hitting children, men hitting women and children—most of the women I talked with not only did not hit but were compulsive about not using physical force.

Overall the process by which women recover from the experience of being hit by loved ones is a complicated and multi-faceted one, an area where there must be much more feminist study and research. To many of us, feminists calling attention to the reality of violence in intimate relationships has not in and of itself compelled most people to take the issue seriously, and such violence seems to be daily on the increase. In this essay, I have raised issues that are not commonly talked about, even among folks who are particularly concerned about violence against women. I hope it will serve as a catalyst for further thought, that it will strengthen our efforts as feminist activists to create a world where domination and coercive abuse are never aspects of intimate relationships.

13

feminism and militarism: a comment

I

As a child growing up in Hopkinsville, Kentucky with its proximity to Fort Campbell, I thought the army was composed primarily of black men. When I saw soldiers, they were black. I overheard adults talking about black men joining the army to find work, to find the dignity that comes with having a purpose in life. They would say, "better to be in the army than prowling the streets." Yet my father cautioned his daughters about entering relationships with soldiers, telling us "he knew what these men were like—he'd been in the army." There was an aspect of his experience serving in the all-black Quartermasters working supply lines during World War II that had changed him profoundly. After returning home, he showed no interest in travelling to new places, to "foreign" lands. An unexplained, unnamed aspect of that experience made him linger near home. I can remember my surprise when I discovered pictures of him in uniform, pictures taken in foreign places about which he never spoke. Yet he always kept a picture of the black men in his section of the 537th Battalion in his room. As children, we often studied the faces of those black men in uniform, looking for him. At age sixty-one, he travelled to Indiana to reunite with his army comrades, to mourn for those dead, to lament that no amount of fighting had brought an end to war.

More than ten years ago, when I first applied to enter college, one school had a special scholarship for relatives of men who had fought in World War I. It was then that I asked my grandfather, Daddy Gus, if he had fought in the war. His voice when he responded was gruff and exasperated, saying, "No. I would have none of war. Why should I have fought in any war. No I never fought nobody's war." Since childhood and into my adulthood, he had loomed large in the landscape of masculinity as a man who truly lived in peace and harmony with those around him—violence was just not his way. His persistent anti-war stance, as well as the anti-war stance of other southern black males in our community who were very vocal about their feelings about militarism (highlighting the contradiction that black men should serve in wars, die for this country, for this democracy, which institutionalized racism and denied them freedom), impressed me. Their attitudes showed us that all men do not glory in war, that all men who fight in wars do not necessarily believe that wars are just, that men are not inherently capable of killing or that militarism is the only possible means of safety. I have thought of these black men often when I hear statements that suggest that men like war, that men wish for the glory of death in war.

Many women who advocate feminism see militarism as exemplifying patriarchal concepts of masculinity and the right of males to dominate others. To these women, struggling against militarism is to struggle against patriarchy. Rena Patterson argued in her essay, "Militarism and the Tradition of Radical Feminism":

> To prevent war is to fight male power, to expose and defy the pretensions of masculinity, and to recognize and act against the basic principles operating in all domains of patriarchal-capitalist society.

Introducing her book of essays *Ain't Nowhere We Can Run: A Handbook For Women on the Nuclear Mentality,* Susan Koen writes:

> It is our belief that the tyranny created by nuclear activities is merely the latest and most serious manifestation of a culture characterized in every shape by domination and exploitation. For this reason, the presence of the nuclear mentality in the world can only be viewed as one part of the whole, not as an isolated issue. We urge the realization that separating the issue of nuclear power plants and weapons from the dominant cultural, social, and political perspective of our society results in a limited understanding of the problem, and in turn limits the range of possible solutions. We offer then, the argument that those male-defined constructs which control our social structure and relationships are directly responsible for the proliferation of nuclear plants and weapons. Patriarchy is the root of the problem, and the imminent dangers created by the nuclear mentality serve to call our attention to the basic problem of patriarchy.

By equating militarism and patriarchy, these feminists often structure their arguments in such a way as to suggest that to be male is synonymous with strength, aggression, and the will to dominate and do violence to others; and that to be female is synonymous with weakness, passivity, and the will to nourish and affirm the lives of others. While these may be stereotypical norms that many people live out, such dualistic thinking is dangerous; it is a basic ideological component of the logic that informs and promotes domination in Western society. Even when inverted and employed for a meaningful purpose, like nuclear disarmament, it is nevertheless risky, for it reinforces the cultural basis of sexism and other forms of group oppression. Suggesting as it does that women and men are inherently different in some fixed and absolute way, it implies that women by virtue of our sex have played no crucial role in supporting and upholding imperialism (and the militarism that serves to maintain imperialist rule) or other systems of domination. Often the women who make such assertions are white. Black women are very likely to feel strongly that white women have been quite violent, militaristic in their support and maintenance of racism.

Rather than clarifying for women the power we exert in the maintenance of systems of domination and setting forth strategies for resistance and change, most current discussions of feminism and militarism further mystify woman's role. In keeping with sexist thinking, women are described as objects rather than subjects. We are depicted not as laborers and activists who, like men, make political choices, but as passive observers who have taken no responsibility for actively maintaining and perpetuating the current value system of our society which privileges violence and domination as the most effective tool of coercive control in human interaction, a society whose value systems advocate and promote war. Discussions of feminism and militarism that do not clarify for women the roles we play in all their variety and complexity, make it appear that all women are against war, that men are the enemy. This is a distortion of woman's reality, not a clarification, not a redefinition.

Such devaluation of the roles women have played necessarily constructs a false notion of female experience. I use the word "devaluation" because it seems that the suggestion that men have made war and war policy represents a refusal to see women as active political beings even though we may be in roles subordinate to men, and the assumption that to be deemed inferior or submissive necessarily defines what one actually is or how one actually continues a sexist pattern that would deny the "powers of the weak," as Elizabeth Janeway labels it. While I think it is important for advocates of feminist movement to continually critique patriarchy, I also think it important that we work to clarify women's political engagements, and not ignore our power to choose to be for or against militarism.

When I hear statements like "women are the natural enemies of war," I am convinced that we are promoting a simplistic view of woman's psyche, of our political reality. Many female anti-war activists suggest that women as bearers of children or the potential bearers of children are necessarily more concerned about war than men. The implication is that mothers are necessarily life-affirming. Leslie Cagan, in an interview in *South End Press News*, confirms that women participating in disarmament work often suggest that because they bear children they have a "special relationship and responsibility to the survival of the planet." Cagan maintains, and rightly so, that this is a "dangerous perspective" because "it focusses on woman's biology and tends to reinforce the sexist notion that womanhood equals motherhood." She explains:

> It may be that some, even many, women are motivated to activism through concern for their children. (It may also be a factor for some fathers who don't want to see their kids blown up in a nuclear war either!). But this simply doesn't justify a narrow and limiting perspective. It is limiting because it says that woman's relationship to such an important issue as the future of our planet rests on a single biological fact.

Advocates of feminism who are concerned about militarism must insist that women (even those who have children) are not inherently more life-affirming or non-violent. Many women who mother are very violent. Many women who mother, either as single parents or with males, have taught male and female children to see fighting and other forms of violent aggression as acceptable modes of communication that are more valued than loving or caring interaction. Even though women often assume a nurturing, life-affirming role in their relationship to others, performing that role does not necessarily mean that they value or respect that mode of relating as much as they may revere the suppression of emotion or the assertion of power through force. Feminists must insist that women who do choose (whether or not they are inspired by motherhood) to denounce violence, domination, and its ultimate expression—war—are political thinkers making political choices. If women who oppose militarism continue to imply, however directly or indirectly, that there is an inherent predisposition in women to hate violence, they risk reinforcing the very biological determinism that has been the ideological stronghold of anti-feminists.

Most importantly, by suggesting that women are naturally nonviolent, anti-war activists mask the reality that masses of women in the United States are not anti-imperialist, are not against militarism, and until their value systems change, they must be seen as clinging, like their male counterparts, to a perspective on human relationships that embraces social domination in all its forms. Imperialism and not patriarchy is the core foundation of militarism. Many societies in the world that are ruled by males are not imperialistic. Nor is it inconceivable in white-supremacist societies like Southern Africa, Australia, and the United States, that sexist men will support continued efforts to equalize the social status of white women and white men to strengthen white supremacy. Throughout the history of the United States, prominent white women who have worked for women's rights have felt no contradiction between this effort and their support of white Western imperialists' attempts to control the planet. Often they argued that more rights for white women would better enable them to support U.S. nationalism and imperialism.

At the beginning of the 20th century, many white women who were strong advocates of women's liberation were pro-imperialist. Books like Helen Barret Montgomery's *Western Women in Eastern Lands,* published in 1910 to document fifty years of women's work in foreign missions, indicate that these women saw no contradiction between their efforts to achieve emancipation of the female sex and their support for the hegemonic spread of Western values and Western domination of the globe. As missionaries, these women, the vast majority of them white, travelled to Eastern lands not as soldiers but nevertheless armed with psychological weapons that would help to perpetuate white supremacy and white Western imperialism. In the closing statement of her work, Helen Montgomery declares:

> So many voices are calling us, so many demand our allegiance, that we are in danger of forgetting the best. To seek first to bring Christ's kingdom on the earth, to respond to the need that is sorest, to go out into the desert for that loved and bewildered sheep that the shepherd has missed from the fold, to share all of privilege with the unprivileged and happiness with the unhappy, to lay down life, if need be, in the Way of the Christ, to see the possibility of one redeemed earth, undivided, unvexed, unperplexed resting in the light of the glorious Gospel of the blessed God, this is the mission of the women's missionary movement.

Like some contemporary feminists, these white women were convinced that they were naturally predisposed to bring nurturance and care, though in this case it was to non-white countries, rather than to anti-war efforts.

It is still true that men more so than women, and white men more so than any other group, advocate militarism, spread imperialism; that men continue to commit the majority of violent acts in war. Yet this sex role division of labor does not necessarily mean that women think differently than men about violence, or would act significantly different if in power. Historically, in times of national crisis, women fight in combat globally and do not show any predisposition to be more nonviolent. Significantly, war does not simply involve the arena of combat. Wars are supported by individuals on a number of fronts. Ideologically, most of us have been raised to believe war is necessary and inevitable. In our daily lives, individuals who have passively accepted this socialization reinforce value systems that support, encourage, and accept violence as a means of social control. Such acceptance is a prerequisite for participation in imperialist struggle and for supporting the militarism that aids such struggle. Women in the United States are taught the same attitudes and values as men, even though sexism assigns us different roles. At the end of an essay discussing women's participation in war efforts, "The Culture in Our Blood," Patty Walton asserts:

> In conclusion, women have not fought in wars because of our material circumstances and not because we are innately more moral than men or because of any biological limitation on our part. The work of women supports both a society's war and its peace activities. And our support has always derived from our particular socialization as women. In fact, the socialization of women and men complements the needs of the culture in which we live... Men are no more innately aggressive than women are passive. We have cultures of war, so we can have cultures of peace.

Sex role division of labor has meant that often as parents, women support war effort by instilling in the minds of children an acceptance of domination and a respect for violence as a means of social control. The sharing of these values is as central to the making of a militaristic state as is the overall control of males by small, ruling groups that insist that men make war and reward their efforts. Like men, women in the United States learn from watching endless hours of television to witness violence without responding. To fight militarism, we must resist the socialization and brainwashing in our culture that teaches passive acceptance of violence in daily life, that teaches us we can eliminate violence with violence. On a small yet significant scale we should all monitor the television watching of children and ourselves. Since bourgeois women in the United States benefit from imperialist conquest as consumers, we must consume less and advocate redistribution of wealth as one way to end militarism. Women who oppose militarism must be willing to withdraw all support for war, knowing full well that such withdrawal necessarily begins with a transformation in our psyches, one that changes our passive acceptance of violence as a means of social control into active resistance.

14

pedagogy and political commitment: a comment

Education is a political issue for exploited and oppressed people. The history of slavery in the United States shows that black people regarded education—book learning, reading, and writing—as a political necessity. Struggle to resist white supremacy and racist attacks informed black attitudes toward education. Without the capacity to read and write, to think critically and analytically, the liberated slave would remain forever bound, dependent on the will of the oppressor. No aspect of black liberation struggle in the United States has been as charged with revolutionary fervor as the effort to gain access to education at all levels.

From slavery to the present, education has been revered in black communities, yet it has also been suspect. Education represented a means of radical resistance but it also led to caste/class divisions between the educated and the uneducated, as it meant the learned black person could more easily adopt the values and attitudes of the oppressor. Education could help one assimilate. If one could not become the white oppressor, one could at least speak and think like him or her, and in some cases the educated black person assumed the role of mediator—explaining uneducated black folks to white folks.

Given this history, many black parents have encouraged children to acquire an education while simultaneously warning us about the danger of education. One very real danger, as many black parents traditionally perceived it, was that the learned black person might lose touch with the concrete reality of everyday black experience. Books and ideas were important but not important enough to become barriers between the individual and community participation. Education was considered to have the potential to alienate one from community and awareness of our collective circumstance as black people. In my family, it was constantly emphasized that too much book learning could lead to madness. Among everyday black folks, madness was deemed to be any loss of one's ability to communicate effectively with others, one's ability to cope with practical affairs.

These ambivalent attitudes toward education have made it difficult for black students to adapt and succeed in educational settings. Many of us have found that to succeed at the very education we had been encouraged to seek, would be most easily accomplished if we separated ourselves from the experience of black folk, the underprivileged experience of the black underclass that was our grounding reality. This ambivalent stance toward education has had a tremendous impact on my psyche. Within the working-class black community where I grew up, I learned to be suspicious of education and suspicious of white folks. I went for my formative educational years to all-black schools. In those schools, I learned about the reality of white people but also about the reality of black people, about our history. We were taught in those schools to be proud of ourselves as black people and to work for the uplift of our race.

Experiencing as I did an educational environment structured to meet our needs as black people, we were deeply affected when those schools ceased to exist and we were compelled to attend white schools instead. At the white school, we were no longer people with a history, a culture. We did not exist as anything other than primitives and slaves. School was no longer the place where one learned how to use education as a means to resist white-supremacist oppression. Small wonder that I spent my last few years of high school depressed about education, feeling as though we had suffered a grave loss, that the direction had shifted, the goals had changed. We were no longer taught by people who spoke our language, who understood our culture; we were taught by strangers. And further, we were dependent on those strangers for evaluation, for approval. We learned not to challenge their racism since they had power over us. Although we were told at home that we were not to openly challenge whites, we were also told not to learn to think like them.

Within this atmosphere of ambivalence toward education, I, who had been dubbed smart, was uncertain about whether or not I wanted to go to college. School was an oppressive drag. Yet the fate of smart black women had already been decided; we would be schoolteachers. At the private, mostly white women's college where I spent my first year, I was an outsider. Determined to stay grounded in the reality of southern black culture, I kept myself aloof from the social practices of the white women with whom

I lived and studied. They, in their turn, perceived me as hostile and alien. I, who had always been a member of a community, was now a loner. One of my white teachers suggested to me that the alienation I experienced was caused by being at a school that was not intellectually challenging, that I should go to Stanford where she had gone.

My undergraduate years at Stanford were difficult ones. Not only did I feel myself alienated from the white people who were my peers and teachers, but I met black people who were different, who did not think the way I did about black culture or black life—who seemed in some ways as strange to me as white people. I had known black people from different classes in my hometown, but we still experienced much the same reality, shared similar world views. It was different at Stanford. I was in an environment where black people's class backgrounds and their values were radically different than my own.

To overcome my feelings of isolation, I bonded with workers, with black women who labored as maids, as secretaries. With them I felt at home. During holiday break, I would stay in their homes. Yet being with them was not the same as being home. In their houses I was an honored guest, someone to be looked up to, because I was getting a college education. My undergraduate years at Stanford were spent struggling to find meaning and significance in education. I had to succeed. I could not let my family or the race down. And so I graduated in English. I had become an English major for the same reason that hundreds of students of all races become English majors: I like to read. Yet I did not fully understand that the study of literature in English departments would really mean the study of works by white males.

It was disheartening for me and other non-white students to face the extent to which education in the university was not the site of openness and intellectual challenge we had longed for. We hated the racism, the sexism, the domination. I began to have grave doubts about the future. Why was I working to be an academic if I did not see people in that environment who were opposing domination? Even those very few concerned professors who endeavored to make courses interesting, to create a learning atmosphere, rarely acknowledged destructive and oppressive aspects of authoritarian rule in and outside the classroom. Whether one took courses from professors with feminist politics or marxist politics, their presentations of self in the classroom never differed from the norm. This was especially so with marxist professors. I asked one of these professors, a white male, how he could expect students to take his politics seriously as a radical alternative to a capitalist structure if we found marxist professors to be even more oppressively authoritarian than other professors. Everyone seemed reluctant to talk about the fact that professors who advocated radical politics rarely allowed their critique of domination and oppression to influence teaching strategies. The absence of any model of a professor who was combining a radical politic opposing domination with practice of that

politic in the classroom made me feel wary about my ability to do differently. When I first began to teach, I tried not to emulate my professors in any
way. I devised different strategies and approaches that I felt were more in
keeping with my politics. Reading the work of Paulo Freire greatly influenced my sense that much was possible in the classroom setting, that
one did not simply need to conform.

In the introduction to a conversation with Paulo Freire published in
idac, emphasis is placed on an educative process that is not based on an
authoritarian, dominating model where knowledge is transferred from a
powerful professor to a powerless student. Education, it was suggested,
could be a space for the development of critical consciousness, where there
could be dialogue and mutual growth of both student and professor:

> If we accept education in this richer and more dynamic sense of ac-
> quiring a critical capacity and intervention in reality, we immediately
> know that there is no such thing as neutral education. All education
> has an intention, a goal, which can only be political. Either it mystifies
> reality by rendering it impenetrable and obscure—which leads people
> to a blind march through incomprehensible labyrinths or it unmasks
> the economic and social structures which are determining the relation-
> ships of exploitation and oppression among persons, knocking down
> labyrinths and allowing people to walk their own road. So we find
> ourselves confronted with a clear option: to educate for liberation or
> to educate for domination.

In retrospect, it seems that my most radical professors were still educating
for domination. And I wondered if this was so because we could not imagine how to educate for liberation in the corporate university. In Freire's
case, he speaks as a white man of privilege who stands and acts in solidarity
with oppressed and exploited groups, especially in their efforts to establish literacy programs that emphasize education for critical consciousness.
In my case, as a black woman from a working-class background, I stand
and act as a member of an oppressed, exploited group, who has managed
to acquire a degree of privilege. While I choose to educate for liberation,
the site of my work has been within the walls of universities peopled lar-
gely by privileged white students and a few non-white students. Within
those walls, I have tried to teach literature and Women's Studies courses
in a way that does not reinforce structures of domination: imperialism,
racism, sexism, and class exploitation.

I do not pretend that my approach is politically neutral, yet this dis-
turbs students who have been led to believe that all education within the
university should be "neutral." On the first day of classes, I talk about my
approach, about the ways the class may be different from other classes as
we work to create strategies of learning to meet our needs—and of course
we must discover together what those needs are. Even though I explain
that the class will be different, students do not always take it seriously. One

central difference is that all students are expected to contribute to class discussion, if not spontaneously, then through the reading of paragraphs and short papers. In this way, every student makes a contribution, every student's voice is heard. Despite the fact that this may be stated at the onset of class, written clearly on the syllabus, students will complain and whine about having to speak. It is only recently that I have begun to see much of the complaining as "change back" behavior. Students and teachers find it hard to shift their paradigms even though they have been longing for a different approach.

Struggling to educate for liberation in the corporate university is a process that I have found enormously stressful. Implementing new teaching strategies that aim to subvert the norm, to engage students fully, is really a difficult task. Unlike the oppressed or colonized, who may begin to feel as they engage in education for critical consciousness a new found sense of power and identity that frees them from colonization of the mind, that liberates, privileged students are often downright unwilling to acknowledge that their minds have been colonized, that they have been learning how to be oppressors, how to dominate, or at least how to passively accept the domination of others. This past teaching year, a student confronted me (a black male student from a middle-class urban experience) in class with the question of what I expected from them (like his tone of voice was: did I have the right to expect anything). Seriously, he wanted to know what I wanted from them. I told him and the class that I thought the most important learning experience that could happen in our classroom was that students would learn to think critically and analytically, not just about the required books, but about the world they live in. Education for critical consciousness that encourages all students—privileged or non-privileged—who are seeking an entry into class privilege rather than providing a sense of freedom and release, invites critique of conventional expectations and desires. They may find such an experience terribly threatening. And even though they may approach the situation with great openness, it may still be difficult, and even painful.

This past semester, I taught a course on black women writers in which students were encouraged to think about the social context in which literature emerges, the impact of politics of domination—racism, sexism, class exploitation—on the writing. Students stated quite openly and honestly that reading the literature in the context of class discussion was making them feel pain. They complained that everything was changing for them, that they were seeing the world differently, and seeing things in that world that were painful to face. Never before had a group of students so openly talked about the way in which learning to see the world critically was causing pain. I did not belittle their pain or try to rationalize it. Initially, I was uncertain about how to respond and just asked us all to think about it. Later, we discussed the way in which all their comments implied that to experience pain is bad, an indication that something is wrong. We talked about changing how we perceive pain, about our society's approach to pain, considering the possibility that this pain could be a constructive sign of growth. I shared with them my sense that the experience should not be viewed as static, that at another point the knowledge and new perspectives they had might lead to clarity and a greater sense of well-being.

Education for liberation can work in the university setting but it does not lead students to feel they are enjoying class or necessarily feeling positive about me as a teacher. One aspect of radical pedagogy that has been difficult for me is learning to cope with not being seen positively by students. When one provides an experience of learning that is challenging, possibly threatening, it is not entertainment, or necessarily a fun experience, though it can be. If one primary function of such a pedagogy is to prepare students to live and act more fully in the world, then it is usually when they are in that context, outside the classroom, that they most feel and experience the value of what they have shared and learned. For me, this often means that most positive feedback I receive as a teacher comes after students have left the class and rarely during it.

Recently, talking with a group of students and faculty at Duke University, we focussed on the issue of exposure and vulnerability. One white male professor, who felt his politics to be radical, his teaching to be an education for liberation, his teaching strategies subversive, felt it was important that no one in the university's bureaucratic structure know what was happening in the classroom. Fear of exposure may lead teachers with radical visions to suppress insight, to follow set norms. Until I came to teach at Yale, no one outside my classes had paid much attention to what was going on inside them. At Yale, students talked a lot outside about my classes, about what happens in them. This was very difficult for me as I felt both exposed and constantly scrutinized. I was certainly subjected to much critical feedback both from students in my classes and faculty and students who heard about them. Their responses forced recognition of the way in which teaching that is overtly political, especially if it radically challenges the status quo, requires acknowledgement that to choose education as the practice of freedom is to take a political stance that may have serious consequences.

Despite negative feedback or pressures, the most rewarding aspect of such teaching is to influence the way students mature and grow intellectually and spiritually. For those students who wish to try to learn in a new way but who have fears, I try to reassure them that their involvement in different types of learning experiences need not threaten their security in other classes; it will not destroy the backing system of education, so they need not panic. Of course, if all they can do is panic, then that is a sign that the course is not for them. My commitment to education as the practice of freedom is strengthened by the large number of students who take my courses and, by doing so, affirm their longing to learn in a new way. Their testimony confirms that education as the practice of liberation does take place in university settings, that our lives are transformed there, that there we do meaningful radical political work.

15

feminist politicization: a comment

Always a part of my inner listening self closes down when I hear the words "the personal is political." Yes, I understand them. I understand that aspect of early feminist consciousness-raising that urged every listening woman to see her problems, especially problems she experienced as the outcome of sexism and sexist oppression, as political issues. To begin on the inside and move outside. To begin with the self as starting point, then to move beyond self-reflection to an awareness of collective reality. This was the promise these words held. But that promise was all too easily un-fulfilled, broken. A culture of domination is necessarily narcissistic. To take woman to the self as starting point for politicization, woman who, in white-supremacist, capitalist patriarchy, is particularly made, socially constructed, to think only me—my body—I constitute a universe—all that truly matters. To take her—this woman—to the self as starting point for politicization is necessarily risky.

We see now the danger in "the personal is political." The personal most known as private, as that space where there is no intervention from the outside, as that which can be kept to the self, as that which does not extend beyond. Knowing the way this culture conceives the personal, the promise was to transform the meaning by linking it with the political, a word so associated in the minds of even small school children with govern-ment, with a world of affairs outside the body, the private, the self. We see now the danger. "The personal is political." No sense of connection between one's person and a larger material reality—no sense of what the political is. In this phrase, what most resonates is the word personal—not the word political. Unsure of the political, each female presumes knowledge of the person—the personal. No need then to search for the meaning of political, simpler to stay with the personal, to make synonymous the personal and the political. Then the self does not become that which one moves into to move beyond, or to connect with. It stays in place, the starting point from which one need never move. If the personal and the political are one and the same, then there is no politicization, no way to become the radical feminist subject.

Perhaps these words are too strong. Perhaps some of you remember the poignancy, the depth, the way this slogan reached into your life, grasped hold of your experience—and you did move. You did understand better the link between personal experience and political reality. The ways individual women were able to concretely find the deep structure of this slogan, use it to radicalize consciousness, need not be denied. Still, to name the danger, the ways it led feminist politics into identity politics, is crucial for the construction of a social space, a radical front wherein politicization of consciousness, of the self, can become real in everyday life.

This slogan had such power because it insisted on the primacy of the personal, not in a narcissistic way, but in its implied naming of the self as a site for politicization, which was in this society a very radical challenge to notions of self and identity. The challenging meaning behind the slogan, however, was not consistently conveyed. While stating "the personal is political" did highlight feminist concern with self, it did not insist on a connection between politicization and transformation of consciousness. It spoke most immediately to the concerns women had about self and identity. Again, the radical insistence on the primacy of a politicized self was submerged, subsumed within a larger cultural framework wherein focus on identity was already legitimized within structures of domination. Obsessive, narcissistic concern with "finding an identity" was already a popular cultural preoccupation, one that deflected attention away from radical politics. Feminist focus on self was then easily linked not to a process of radical politicization, but to a process of de-politicization. Popularly, the important quest was not to radically change our relationship to self and identity, to educate for critical consciousness, to become politically engaged and committed, but to explore one's identity, to affirm and assert the primacy of the self as it already existed. Such a focus was strengthened by an emphasis within feminist movement on lifestyle, on being politically correct in one's representation of self rather than being political.

Exasperated with identity politics, Jenny Bourne begins her essay, "Homelands of the Mind: Jewish Feminism and Identity Politics," with the assertion:

Identity Politics is all the rage. Exploitation is out (it is extrinsically determinist). Oppression is in (it is intrinsically personal). What is to be done has been replaced by who am I. Political culture has ceded to cultural politics. The material world has passed into the metaphysical. The Blacks, the Women, the Gays have all searched for themselves. And now combining all their quests, has arrived the quest for Jewish feminist identity.

Bourne's essay speaks to the crisis of political commitment and engagement engendered by relentless focus on identity. I wholeheartedly affirm her effort to expose the ways identity politics has led to the construction of a notion of feminist movement that is, as she sees it, "separatist, individualistic, and inward-looking." She asserts: "The organic relationship we tried to forge between the personal and the political has been so degraded that now the only area of politics deemed legitimate is the personal." However, I think it essential not to mock or ridicule the metaphysical but to find a constructive point of connection between material struggle and metaphysical concerns. We cannot oppose the emphasis on identity politics by inverting the logic and devaluing the personal. It does not further feminist movement to ignore issues of identity or to critique concern with self without posing alternative approaches, without addressing in a dialectical manner the issue of feminist politicization—the link between efforts to socially construct self, identity in an oppositional framework, one that resists domination, and allows for the greatest degree of well-being.

To challenge identity politics we must offer strategies of politicization that enlarge our conception of who we are, that intensify our sense of intersubjectivity, our relation to a collective reality. We do this by reemphasizing how history, political science, psychoanalysis, and diverse ways of knowing can be used to inform our ideas of self and identity. Politicization of the self can have its starting point in an exploration of the personal wherein what is first revolutionized is the way we think about the self. To begin revisioning, we must acknowledge the need to examine the self from a new, critical standpoint. Such a perspective, while it would insist on the self as a site for politicization, would equally insist that simply describing one's experience of exploitation or oppression is not to become politicized. It is not sufficient to know the personal but to know—to speak it in a different way. Knowing the personal might mean naming spaces of ignorance, gaps in knowledge, ones that render us unable to link the personal with the political.

In *Ain't I a Woman,* I pointed to the distinction between experiencing a form of exploitation and understanding the particular structure of domination that is the cause. The opening paragraph of the chapter on "Racism and Feminism: The Issue of Accountability" begins:

American women of all races are socialized to think of racism solely in the context of race hatred. Specifically in the case of black and white people. For most women, the first knowledge of racism as institution-alized oppression is engendered either by direct personal experience or through information gleaned from conversations, books, television, or movies. Consequently, the American woman's understanding of racism as a political tool of colonialism and imperialism is severely limited. To experience the pain of race hatred or to witness that pain is not to understand its origin, evolution, or impact on world history.

Many women engaged in feminist movement assumed that describing one's personal experience of exploitation by men was to be politicized. Politiciza-tion necessarily combines this process (the naming of one's experience) with critical understanding of the concrete material reality that lays the groundwork for that personal experience. The work of understanding that groundwork and what must be done to transform it is quite different from the effort to raise one's consciousness about personal experience even as they are linked.

Feminist critiques of identity politics which call attention to the way it undermines feminist movement should not deny the importance of naming and giving voice to one's experience. It must be continually stressed that this is only part of the process of politicization, one which must be linked to education for critical consciousness that teaches about structures of domination and how they function. It is understanding the latter that enables us to imagine new possibilities, strategies for change and transfor-mation. The extent to which we are able to link radical self-awareness to collective struggle to change and transform self and society will determine the fate of feminist revolution.

Focus on self in feminist movement has not been solely the province of privileged white women. Women of color, many of whom were strug-gling to articulate and name our experience for the first time, also began to focus attention on identity in static and non-productive ways. Jenny Bourne focusses on individual black women who promoted identity politics, calling attention to a statement by the Combahee River Collective which reads: "The most profound and potentially the most radical politics come directly out of our own identity as opposed to working to end some-body else's oppression." This statement asserts the primacy of identity politics. Coming from radical black women, it served to legitimize the em-phasis in feminist movement on identity—that to know one's needs as an individual is to be political. It is in many ways a very problematic state-ment. If one's identity is constructed from a base of power and privilege gained from participation in and acceptance of structures of domination, it is not a given that focus on naming that identity will lead to a radicalized consciousness, a questioning of that privilege, or to active resistance. It is possible to name one's personal experience without committing oneself to transforming or changing that experience.

To imply, as this statement does, that individuals cannot successful-ly radicalize their consciousness and their actions as much by working in resistance struggles that do not directly effect their lives is to underestimate the power of solidarity. It is only as allies with those who are exploited and oppressed, working in struggles for liberation, that individuals who are not victimized demonstrate their allegiance, their political commitment, their determination to resist, to break with the structures of domination that offer them personal privilege. This holds true for individuals from oppressed and exploited groups as well. Our consciousness can be radicalized by acting to eradicate forms of domination that do not have direct correspondence with our identities and experiences. Bourne states:

> Identity politics regards the discovery of identity as its supreme goal. Feminists even assert that discovering an identity is an act of resistance. The mistake is to view identity as an end rather than a means... Identity is not merely a precursor to action, it is also created through action.

Indeed, for many exploited and oppressed peoples the struggle to create an identity, to name one's reality is an act of resistance because the process of domination—whether it be imperialist colonization, racism, or sexist oppression—has stripped us of our identity, devalued language, culture, appearance. Again, this is only a stage in the process of revolution (one Bourne seems to deny has any value), but it must not be denigrated, even if people of privilege repeat this gesture so often that it has no radical implications. For example: the slogan "black is beautiful" was an important popular expression of resistance to white supremacy (of course that expression loses meaning and power if it is not linked to a process of politicization where black people learn to see ourselves as subjects rather than as objects, where as an expression of being subjects we act to transform the world we live in so that our skin no longer signifies that we will be degraded, exploited). It would be a grave mistake to suggest that politicization of self is not part of the process by which we prepare ourselves to act most effectively for radical social change. Only when it becomes narcissistic or when, as Bourne states, it naively suggests that "structural, material issues of race, class, and power, would first be resolved in terms of personal consciousness" does it diminish liberatory struggle.

When I chart a map of feminist politicization, of how we become more politically self-aware, I begin with the insistence on commitment to education for critical consciousness. Much of that education does start with examining the self from a new, critical perspective. To this end, confession and memory can be used constructively to illuminate past experiences, particularly when such experience is theorized. Using confession and memory as ways of naming reality enables women and men to talk about personal experience as part of a process of politicization which places such talk in a dialectical context. This allows us to discuss personal experience in a different way, in a way that politicizes not just the telling, but the tale. Theorizing experience as we tell personal narrative, we have a sharper, keener sense of the end that is desired by the telling. An interesting and constructive use of memory and confession is narrated in the book, *Female Sexualization: A Collective Work of Memory,* edited by Frigga Haug. Collectively, the women who speak work not just to name their experience but to place that experience in a theoretical context. They use confession and memory as tools of intervention which allow them to unite scientific knowledge with everyday experience. So as not to place undue emphasis on the individual, they consistently link individual experience to collective reality. Story-telling becomes a process of historicization. It does not remove women from history but enables us to see ourselves as part of history. The act of writing autobiographical stories enabled the women in the Haug book to see themselves form a different perspective, one which they describe as a "politically necessary form of cultural labor." They comment, "It makes us live our lives more consciously." Used constructively, confession and memory are tools that heighten self-awareness; they need not make us solely inward-looking.

Feminist thinkers in the United States use confession and memory primarily as a way to narrate tales of victimization, which are rarely rendered dialectically. This focus means that we do not have various and diverse accountings of all aspects of female experience. As we struggle to learn more about how women relate to one another, to men, and to children in everyday life, how we construct strategies of resistance and survival, it is useful to rely on confession and memory as documentary sources. We must, however, be careful not to promote the construction of narratives of female experience that become so normative that all experience that does not fit the model is deemed illegitimate or unworthy of investigation.

Rethinking ways to constructively use confession and memory shifts the focus away from mere naming of one's experience. It enables feminist thinkers to talk about identity in relation to culture, history, politics, whatever and to challenge the notion of identity as static and unchanging. To explore identity in relation to strategies of politicization, feminist thinkers must be willing to see the female self anew, to examine how we are gendered critically and analytically from various standpoints. In early feminist consciousness-raising, confession was often the way to share negative traumas, the experience of male violence for example. Yet there remain many unexplored areas of female experience that need to be fully examined, thereby widening the scope of our understanding of what it is to be female in this society. Imagine a group of black women working to educate ourselves for critical consciousness, exploring our relation to radical politics, to left politics. We might better understand our collective reluctance to commit ourselves to feminist struggle, to revolutionary politics or we might also chart those experiences that prepare and enable us to make such commitments.

There is much exciting work to be done when we use confession and memory as a way to theorize experience, to deepen our awareness, a s part of the process of radical politicization. Often we experience pleasure and joy when we share personal stories, closeness, intimacy. This is why the personal has had such a place in feminist discourse. To reaffirm the power of the personal while simultaneously not getting trapped in identity politics, we must work to link personal narratives with knowledge of how we must act politically to change and transform the world.

16

overcoming white supremacy: a comment

Black people in the United States share with black people in South Africa and with people of color globally both the pain of white-supremacist oppression and exploitation and the pain that comes from resistance and struggle. The first pain wounds us, the second pain helps heal our wounds. It often troubles me that black people in the United States have not risen *en masse* to declare solidarity with our black sisters and brothers in South Africa. Perhaps one day soon—say Martin Luther King's birthday—we will enter the streets at a certain hour, wherever we are, to stand for a moment, naming and affirming the primacy of black liberation.

As I write, I try to remember when the word racism ceased to be the term which best expressed for me exploitation of black people and other people of color in this society and when I began to understand that the most useful term was white supremacy. It was certainly a necessary term when confronted with the liberal attitudes of white women active in feminist movement who were unlike their racist ancestors—white women in the early woman's rights movement who did not wish to be caught dead in fellowship with black women. In fact, these women often requested and longed for the presence of black women. Yet when present, what we saw was that they wished to exercise control over our bodies and thoughts as their racist ancestors had—that this need to exercise power over us expressed how much they had internalized the values and attitudes of white supremacy.

It may have been this contact or contact with fellow white English professors who want very much to have "a" black person in "their" department as long as that person thinks and acts like them, shares their values and beliefs, is in no way different, that first compelled me to use the term white supremacy to identify the ideology that most determines how white people in this society (irrespective of their political leanings to the right or left) perceive and relate to black people and other people of color. It is the very small but highly visible liberal movement away from the perpetuation of overtly racist discrimination, exploitation, and oppression of black people which often masks how all-pervasive white supremacy is in this society, both as ideology and as behavior. When liberal whites fail to understand how they can and/or do embody white-supremacist values and beliefs even though they may not embrace racism as prejudice or domination (especially domination that involves coercive control), they cannot recognize the ways their actions support and affirm the very structure of racist domination and oppression that they profess to wish to see eradicated.

Likewise, "white supremacy" is a much more useful term for understanding the complicity of people of color in upholding and maintaining racial hierarchies that do not involve force (i.e. slavery, apartheid) than the term "internalized racism"—a term most often used to suggest that black people have absorbed negative feelings and attitudes about blackness held by white people. The term "white supremacy" enables us to recognize not only that black people are socialized to embody the values and attitudes of white supremacy, but that we can exercise "white-supremacist control" over other black people. This is important, for unlike the term "uncle tom," which carried with it the recognition of complicity and internalized racism, a new terminology must accurately name the way we as black people directly exercise power over one another when we perpetuate white-supremacist beliefs. Speaking about changing perspectives on black identity, writer Toni Morrison said in a recent interview: "Now people choose their identities. Now people choose to be Black." At this historical moment, when a few black people no longer experience the racial apartheid and brutal racism that still determine the lot of many black people, it is easier for that few to ally themselves politically with the dominant racist white group.

Assimilation is the strategy that has provided social legitimation for this shift in allegiance. It is a strategy deeply rooted in the ideology of white supremacy and its advocates urge black people to negate blackness, to imitate racist white people so as to better absorb their values, their way of life. Ironically, many changes in social policy and social attitudes that were once seen as ways to end racial domination have served to reinforce and perpetuate white supremacy. This is especially true of social policy that has encouraged and promoted racial integration. Given the continued force of racism, racial integration translated into assimilation ultimately serves to reinforce and maintain white supremacy. Without an ongoing active movement to end white supremacy, without ongoing black liberation struggle, no social environment can exist in the United States that truly supports integration. When black people enter social contexts that remain unchanged, unaltered, in no way stripped of the framework of white supremacy, we are pressured to assimilate. We are rewarded for assimilation. Black people working or socializing in predominately white settings whose very structures are informed by the principles of white supremacy who dare to affirm blackness, love of black culture and identity, do so at great risk. We must continually challenge, protest, resist while working to leave no gaps in our defense that will allow us to be crushed. This is especially true in work settings where we risk being fired or not receiving deserved promotions. Resisting the pressure to assimilate is a part of our struggle to end white supremacy.

When I talk with audiences around the United States about feminist issues of race and gender, my use of the term "white supremacy" always sparks a reaction, usually of a critical or hostile nature. Individual white people and even some non-whites insist that this is not a white-supremacist society, that racism is not nearly the problem it used to be (it is downright frightening to hear people argue vehemently that the problem of racism has been solved), that there has been change. While it is true that the nature of racist oppression and exploitation has changed as slavery has ended and the apartheid structure of Jim Crow has legally changed, white supremacy continues to shape perspectives on reality and to inform the social status of black people and all people of color. Nowhere is this more evident than in university settings. And often it is the liberal folks in those settings who are unwilling to acknowledge this truth.

Recently in a conversation with a white male lawyer at his home where I was a guest, he informed me that someone had commented to him that children are learning very little history these days in school, that the attempt to be all-inclusive, to talk about Native Americans, blacks, women, etc. has led to a fragmented focus on particular representative individuals with no larger historical framework. I responded to this comment by suggesting that it has been easier for white people to practice this inclusion rather than change the larger framework; that it is easier to change the focus from Christopher Columbus, the important white man who "discovered" America, to Sitting Bull or Harriet Tubman, than it is to cease telling a distorted version of U.S. history which upholds white supremacy. Really teaching history in a new way would require abandoning the old myths informed by white supremacy like the notion that Columbus discovered America. It would mean talking about imperialism, colonization, about the Africans who came here before Columbus (see Ivan Van Sertima's *They Came Before Columbus*). It would mean talking about genocide, about the white colonizers' exploitation and betrayal of Native American Indians; about ways the legal and governmental structures of this society from the Constitution on supported and upheld slavery, apartheid (see Derrick Bell's *And We Are Not Saved*). This history can be taught only when the perspectives of teachers are no longer shaped by white supremacy. Our conversation is one of many examples that reveal the way black people and white people can socialize in a friendly manner, be racially integrated, while deeply ingrained notions of white supremacy remain intact. Incidents like this make it necessary for concerned folks, for righteous white people, to begin to fully explore the way white supremacy determines how they see the world, even as their actions are not informed by the type of racial prejudice that promotes overt discrimination and separation.

Significantly, assimilation was a term that began to be more commonly used after the revolts against white supremacy in the late 1960s and early 1970s. The intense, passionate rebellion against racism and white supremacy of this period was crucial because it created a context for politicization, for education for critical consciousness, one in which black people could begin to confront the extent of our complicity, our internalization of white supremacy and begin the process of self-recovery and collective renewal. Describing this effort in his work, *The Search for a Common Ground*, black theologian Howard Thurman commented:

> "Black is Beautiful" became not merely a phrase—it was a stance, a total attitude, a metaphysics. In very positive and exciting terms it began undermining the idea that had developed over so many years into a central aspect of white mythology: that black is ugly, black is evil, black is demonic. In so doing it fundamentally attacked the front line of the defense of the myth of white supremacy and superiority.

Clearly, assimilation as a social policy upholding white supremacy was strategically an important counter-defense, one that would serve to deflect the call for radical transformation of black consciousness. Suddenly the terms for success (that is getting a job, acquiring the means to provide materially for oneself and one's family) were redefined. It was not enough for black people to enter institutions of higher education and acquire the necessary skills to effectively compete for jobs previously occupied solely by whites; the demand was that blacks become "honorary whites," that black people assimilate to succeed.

The force that gave the social policy of assimilation power to influence and change the direction of black liberation struggle was economic. Economic distress created a climate wherein militancy—overt resistance to white supremacy and racism (which included the presentation of self in a manner that suggests black pride)—was no longer deemed a viable survival strategy. Natural hair styles, African dress, etc. were discarded as signs of militancy that might keep one from getting ahead. A similar regressive, reactionary move was taking place among young white radicals, many of whom had been fiercely engaged in left politics, who suddenly began to seek reincorporation into the liberal and conservative mainstream. Again the force behind their re-entry into the system was economic. On a very basic level, changes in the cost of housing (as in the great apartment one had in 1965 for $100 a month cost $400 by 1975) had a frightening impact on college-educated young people of all ethnicities who thought they were committed to transforming society, but who were unable to face living without choice, without the means to escape, who feared living in poverty. Coupled with economic forces exerting pressure, many radicals despaired of the possibility that this white-supremacist, capitalist patriarchy could really be changed.

Tragically, many radical whites who had been allies in the black liberation struggle began to question whether the struggle to end racism was really that significant, or to suggest that the struggle was over, as they moved into their new liberal positions. Radical white youth who had worked in civil rights struggles, protested the war in Vietnam, and even denounced U.S. imperialism could not reconstruct their ties to prevailing systems of domination without creating a new layer of false consciousness—the assertion that racism was no longer pervasive, that race was no longer an important issue. Similarly, critiques of capitalism, especially those that urged individuals to try and live differently within the framework of capitalism, were also relegated to the back burner as people "discovered" that it was important to have class privilege so that one could better help the exploited.

It is no wonder that black radicals met these betrayals with despair and hopelessness. What had all the contemporary struggle to resist racism really achieved? What did it mean to have this period of radical questioning of white supremacy, of black is beautiful, only to witness a few years later the successful mass production by white corporations of hair care products to straighten black hair? What did it mean to witness the assault on black culture by capitalist forces which stress the production on all fronts of an image, a cultural product that can "cross over"—that is, that can speak more directly to the concerns, to the popular imagination of white consumers, while still attracting the dollars of black consumers. And what does it mean in 1987 when television viewers watch a morning talk show on black beauty, where black women suggest that these trends are only related to personal preferences and have no relation to racism; when viewers witness a privileged white male, Phil Donahue, shaking his head and trying to persuade the audience to acknowledge the reality of racism and its impact on black people? Or what does it mean when many black people say that what they like most about the Bill Cosby show is that there is little emphasis on blackness, that they are "just people"? And again to hear reported on national news that little black children prefer playing with white dolls rather than black dolls? All these popular narratives remind us that "we are not yet saved," that white supremacy prevails, that the racist oppression and exploitation which daily assaults the bodies and spirits of black people in South Africa, assaults black people here.

Years ago when I was a high school student experiencing racial desegregation, there was a current of resistance and militancy that was so fierce. It swept over and through our bodies as we—black students—stood, pressed against the red brick walls, watching the national guard with their guns, waiting for those moments when we would enter, when we would break through racism, waiting for the moments of change—of victory. And now even within myself I find that spirit of militancy growing faint; all too often it is assaulted by feelings of despair and powerlessness. I find that I must work to nourish it, to keep it strong. Feelings of despair and power-lessness are intensified by all the images of black self-hate that indicate that those militant 1960s did not have sustained radical impact—that the politicization and transformation of black consciousness did not become an ongoing revolutionary practice in black life. This causes such frustration and despair because it means that we must return to this basic agenda, that we must renew efforts at politicization, that we must go over old ground. Perhaps what is more disheartening is the fear that the seeds, though planted again, will never survive, will never grow strong. Right now it is anger and rage (see Audre Lorde's "The Uses of Anger" in *Sister Outsider*) at the continued racial genocide that rekindles within me that spirit of militancy.

Like so many radical black folks who work in university settings, I often feel very isolated. Often we work in environments predominately peopled by white folks (some of whom are well-meaning and concerned) who are not committed to working to end white supremacy, or who are unsure about what that commitment means. Certainly feminist movement has been one of the places where there has been renewed interest in challenging and resisting racism. There too it has been easier for white women to confront racism as overt exploitation and domination, or as personal prejudice, than to confront the encompassing and profound reality of white supremacy.

In talking about race and gender recently, the question most often asked by white women has to do with white women's response to black women or women of color insisting that they are not willing to teach them about their racism—to show the way. They want to know: What should a white person do who is attempting to resist racism? It is problematic to assert that black people and other people of color who are sincerely committed to struggling against white supremacy should be unwilling to help or teach white people. Challenging black folks in the 19th century, Frederick Douglass made the crucial point that "power accedes nothing without demand." For the racially oppressed to demand of white people, of black people, of all people that we eradicate white supremacy, that those who benefit materially by exercising white-supremacist power, either actively or passively, willingly give up that privilege in response to that demand, and then to refuse to show the way is to undermine our own cause. We must show the way. There must exist a paradigm, a practical model for social change that includes an understanding of ways to transform consciousness that are linked to efforts to transform structures.

Fundamentally, it is our collective responsibility as radical black people and people of color, and as white people to construct models for social change. To abdicate that responsibility, to suggest that change is just something an individual can do on his or her own or in isolation with other racist white people is utterly misleading. If as a black person I say to a white person who shows a willingness to commit herself or himself to the struggle to end white supremacy that I refuse to affirm, or help in that endeavor is a gesture that undermines my commitment to that struggle. Many black people have essentially responded in this way because we do not want to do the work for white people, and most importantly we cannot do the work, yet this often seems to be what is asked of us. Rejecting the work does not mean that we cannot and do not show the way by our actions, by the information we share. Those white people who want to continue the dominate/subordinate relationship so endemic to racist exploitation by insisting that we "serve" them—that we do the work of challenging and changing their consciousness—are acting in bad faith. In his work, *Pedagogy in Progress: The Letters to Guinea-Bissau,* Paulo Freire reminds us:

> Authentic help means that all who are involved help each other mutually, growing together in the common effort to understand the reality which they seek to transform.

It is our collective responsibility as people of color and as white people who are committed to ending white supremacy to help one another. It is our collective responsibility to educate for critical consciousness. If I commit myself politically to black liberation struggle, to the struggle to end white supremacy, I am not making a commitment to working only for and with black people, I must engage in struggle with all willing comrades to strengthen our awareness and our resistance. (See *The Autobiography of Malcolm X* and *The Last Year of Malcolm X—The Evolution of a Revolutionary* by George Breitman.) Malcolm X is an important role model for those of us who wish to transform our consciousness for he was engaged in ongoing critical self-reflection, in changing both his words and his deeds. In thinking about black response to white people, about what they can do to end racism, I am reminded of that memorable example when Malcolm X expressed regret about an incident with a white female college student who asked him what she could do and he told her: "nothing." He later saw that there was much that she could have done. For each of us, it is work to educate ourselves to understand the nature of white supremacy with a critical consciousness. Black people are not born into this world with innate understanding of racism and white supremacy. (See John Hodge, ed., *Cultural Bases of Racism and Group Oppression*.)

In recent years, particularly among women active in feminist movement, much effort to confront racism has focussed on individual prejudice. While it is important that individuals work to transform their consciousness, striving to be anti-racist, it is important for us to remember that the struggle to end white supremacy is a struggle to change a system, a structure. Hodge emphasizes in his book "the problem of racism is not prejudice but domination." For our efforts to end white supremacy to be truly effective, individual struggle to change consciousness must be fundamentally linked to collective effort to transform those structures that reinforce and perpetuate white supremacy.

homophobia in black communities

Recently I was at my parents' home and heard teenage nieces and nephews expressing their hatred for homosexuals, saying that they could never like anybody who was homosexual. In response I told them, "There are already people who you love and care about who are gay, so just come off it!" They wanted to know who. I said, "The who is not important. If they wanted you to know, they would tell you. But you need to think about the shit you've been saying and ask yourself where it's coming from."

Their vehement expression of hatred startled and frightened me, even more so when I contemplated the hurt that would have been experienced had our loved ones who are gay heard their words. When we were growing up, we would not have had the nerve to make such comments. We were not allowed to say negative, hateful comments about the people we knew who were gay. We knew their names, their sexual preference. They were our neighbors, our friends, our family. They were us—a part of our black community.

The gay people we knew then did not live in separate subcultures, not in the small, segregated black community where work was difficult to find, where many of us were poor. Poverty was important; it created a social context in which structures of dependence were important for everyday survival. Sheer economic necessity and fierce white racism, as well as the joy of being there with the black folks known and loved, compelled many gay blacks to live close to home and family. That meant however that gay people created a way to live out sexual preferences within the boundaries of circumstances that were rarely ideal no matter how affirming. In some cases, this meant a closeted sexual life. In other families, an individual could be openly expressive, quite out.

The homophobia expressed by my nieces and nephews coupled with the assumption in many feminist circles that black communities are somehow more homophobic than other communities in the United States, more opposed to gay rights, provided the stimulus for me to write this piece. Initially, I considered calling it "homophobia in the black community." Yet it is precisely the notion that there is a monolithic black community that must be challenged. Black communities vary—urban and rural experiences create diversity of culture and lifestyle.

I have talked with black folks who were raised in southern communities where gay people were openly expressive of their sexual preference and participated fully in the life of the community. I have also spoken with folks who say just the opposite.

In the particular black community where I was raised there was a real double standard. Black male homosexuals were often known, were talked about, were seen positively, and played important roles in community life, whereas lesbians were talked about solely in negative terms, and the women identified as lesbians were usually married. Often, acceptance of male homosexuality was mediated by material privilege—that is to say that homosexual men with money were part of the materially privileged ruling black group and were accorded the regard and respect given that group. They were influential people in the community. This was not the case with any women.

In those days homophobia directed at lesbians was rooted in deep religious and moral belief that women defined their womanness through bearing children. The prevailing assumption was that to be a lesbian was "unnatural" because one would not be participating in child-bearing. There were no identified lesbian "parents" even though there were gay men known to be caretakers of other folks' children. I have talked with black folks who recall similar circumstances in their communities. Overall, a majority of older black people I spoke with, raised in small, tightly knit southern black communities, suggested there was tolerance and acceptance of different sexual practices and preferences. One black gay male I spoke with felt that it was more important for him to live within a supportive black community, where his sexual preferences were known but not acted out in an overt, public way, than to live away from a community in a gay subculture where this aspect of his identity could be openly expressed.

Recently, I talked with a black lesbian from New Orleans who boasted that the black community has never had any "orange person like Anita Bryant running around trying to attack gay people." Her experience coming out to a black male roommate was positive and caring. But for every positive story one might hear about gay life in black communities, there are also negative ones. Yet these positive accounts call into question the assumption that black people and black communities are necessarily more homophobic than other groups of people in this society. They also compel us to recognize that there are diversities of black experience. Unfortunately, there are very few oral histories and autobiographies which explore the lives of black gay people in diverse black communities. This is a research project that must be carried out if we are to fully understand the complex experience of being black and gay in this white-supremacist, patriarchal, capitalist society. Often we hear more from black gay people who have chosen to live in predominantly white communities, whose choices may have been affected by undue harassment in black communities. We hear hardly anything from black gay people who live contentedly in black communities.

Black communities may be perceived as more homophobic than other communities because there is a tendency for individuals in black communities to verbally express in an outspoken way anti-gay sentiments. I talked with a straight black male in a California community who acknowledged that though he has often made jokes poking fun at gays or expressing contempt, as a means of bonding in group settings, in his private life he was a central support person for a gay sister. Such contradictory behavior seems pervasive in black communities. It speaks to ambivalence about sexuality in general, about sex as a subject of conversation, and to ambivalent feelings and attitudes toward homosexuality. Various structures of emotional and economic dependence create gaps between attitudes and actions. Yet a distinction must be made between black people overtly expressing prejudice toward homosexuals and homophobic white people who never make homophobic comments but who have the power to actively exploit and oppress gay people in areas of housing, employment, etc. While both groups perpetuate and reinforce each other and this cannot be denied or downplayed, the truth is that the greatest threat to gay rights does not reside in black communities.

It is far more likely that homophobic attitudes can be altered or changed in environments where they have not become rigidly institutionalized. Rather than suggesting that black communities are more homophobic than other communities, and dismissing them, it is important for feminist activists (especially black folks) to examine the nature of that homophobia, to challenge it in constructive ways that lead to change. Clearly religious beliefs and practices in many black communities promote and encourage homophobia. Many Christian black folks (like other Christians in this society) are taught in churches that it is a sin to be gay, ironically sometimes by ministers who are themselves gay or bisexual.

In the past year I talked with a black woman Baptist minister, who, although concerned about feminist issues, expressed very negative attitudes about homosexuality, because, she explained, the Bible teaches that it is wrong. Yet in her daily life she is tremendously supportive and caring of gay friends. When I asked her to explain this contradiction, she argued that it was not a contradiction, that the Bible also teaches her to identify with those who are exploited and oppressed, and to demand that they be treated justly. To her way of thinking, committing a sin did not mean that one should be exploited or oppressed.

The contradictions, the homophobic attitudes that underlie her attitudes, indicate that there is a great need for progressive black theologians to examine the role black churches play in encouraging persecution of gay people. Individual members of certain churches in black communities should protest when worship services become a platform for teaching anti-gay sentiments. Often individuals sit and listen to preachers raging against gay people and think the views expressed are amusing and outmoded, and dismiss them without challenge. But if homophobia is to be eradicated in black communities, such attitudes must be challenged.

Recently, especially as black people all over the United States discussed the film version of Alice Walker's novel *The Color Purple,* as well as the book itself (which includes a positive portrayal of two black women being sexual with each other), the notion that homosexuality threatens the continuation of black families seems to have gained new momentum. In some cases, black males in prominent positions, especially those in media, have helped to perpetuate this notion. Tony Brown stated in one editorial, "No lesbian relationship can take the place of a positive love relationship between black women and black men." It is both a misreading of Walker's novel and an expression of homophobia for any reader to project into this work the idea that lesbian relationships exist as a competitive response to heterosexual encounters. Walker suggests quite the contrary.

Just a few weeks ago I sat with two black women friends eating bagels as one of us expressed her intense belief that white people were encouraging black people to be homosexuals so as to further divide black folks. She was attributing the difficulties many professional heterosexual black women have finding lovers, companions, husbands, to homosexuality. We listened to her and then the other woman said, "Now you know we are not going to sit here and listen to this homophobic bull without challenging it."

We pointed to the reality that many black gay people are parents, hence their sexual preference does not threaten the continuation of black families. We stressed that many black gay people have white lovers and that there is no guarantee that were they heterosexual they would be partnered with other black people. We argued that people should be able to choose and claim the sexual preference that best expresses their being, suggesting that while it is probably true that positive portrayals of gay people encourage people to see this as a viable sexual preference or lifestyle, it is equally true that compulsory heterosexuality is promoted to a far greater extent. We suggested that we should all be struggling to create a climate where there is freedom of sexual expression.

She was not immediately persuaded by our arguments, but at least she had different perspectives to consider. Supporters of gay rights in black communities must recognize that education for critical consciousness that explains and critiques prevailing stereotypes is necessary for us to eradicate homophobia. A central myth that must be explored and addressed is the notion that homosexuality means genocide for black families. And in conjunction with discussions of this issue, black people must confront the reality of bisexuality and the extent to which the spread of AIDS in black communities is connected to bisexual transmission of the HIV virus.

To strengthen solidarity between black folks irrespective of our sexual preferences, allegiance must be discussed. This is especially critical as more and more black gay people live outside black communities. Just as black women are often compelled to answer the question—which is more important: feminist movement or black liberation struggle?—women's rights or civil rights?—which are you first: black or female?—gay people face similar questions. Are you more identified with the political struggle of your race and ethnic group or gay rights struggle? This question is not a simple one. For some people it is raised in such a way that they are compelled to choose one identity over another.

In one case, when a black family learned of their daughter's lesbianism, they did not question her sexual preference (saying they weren't stupid, they had known she was gay), but the racial identity of her lovers. Why white women and not black women? Her gayness, expressed exclusively in relationships with white women, was deemed threatening because it was perceived as estranging her from blackness.

Little is written about this struggle. Often black families who can acknowledge and accept gayness find inter-racial coupling harder to accept. Certainly among black lesbians, the issue of black women preferring solely white lovers is discussed but usually in private conversation. These relationships, like all cross-racial intimate relationships are informed by the dynamics of racism and white supremacy. Black lesbians have spoken about absence of acknowledgement of one another at social gatherings where the majority of black women present are with white women lovers. Unfortunately, such incidents reinforce the notion that one must choose between solidarity with one's ethnic group and solidarity with those with whom one shares sexual preference, irrespective of class and ethnic difference or differences in political perspective.

Black liberation struggle and gay liberation struggle are both undermined when these divisions are promoted and encouraged. Both gay and straight black people must work to resist the politics of domination as expressed in sexism and racism that lead people to think that supporting one liberation struggle diminishes one's support for another or stands one in opposition to another. As part of education for critical consciousness in black communities, it must be continually stressed that our struggle against racism, our struggle to recover from oppression and exploitation are inex-

tricably linked to all struggles to resist domination—including gay liberation struggle.

Often black people, especially non-gay folks, become enraged when
they hear a white person who is gay suggest that homosexuality is
synonymous with the suffering people experience as a consequence of racial exploitation and oppression. The need to make gay experience and
black experience of oppression synonymous seems to be one that surfaces
much more in the minds of white people. Too often, it is seen as a way of
minimizing or diminishing the particular problems people of color face in
a white-supremacist society, especially the problems encountered because
one does not have white skin. Many of us have been in discussions where
a non-white person—a black person—struggles to explain to white folks
that while we can acknowledge that gay people of all colors are harassed
and suffer exploitation and domination, we also recognize that there is a
significant difference that arises because of the visibility of dark skin. Often
homophobic attacks on gay people occur in situations where knowledge
of sexual preference is indicated or established—outside of gay bars, for
example. While it in no way lessens the severity of such suffering for gay
people, or the fear that it causes, it does mean that in a given situation the
apparatus of protection and survival may be simply not identifying as gay.

In contrast, most people of color have no choice. No one can hide,
change, or mask dark skin color. White people, gay and straight, could
show greater understanding of the impact of racial oppression on people
of color by not attempting to make these oppressions synonymous, but
rather by showing the ways they are linked and yet differ. Concurrently,
the attempt by white people to make synonymous experience of
homophobic aggression with racial oppression deflects attention away from
the particular dual dilemma that non-white gay people face, as individuals
who confront both racism and homophobia.

Often black gay folk feel extremely isolated because there are tensions in their relationships with the larger, predominately white gay community created by racism, and tensions within black communities around
issues of homophobia. Sometimes, it is easier to respond to such tensions
by simply withdrawing from both groups, by refusing to participate or identify oneself politically with any struggle to end domination. By affirming
and supporting black people who are gay within our communities, as well
as outside our communities, we can help reduce and change the pain of
such isolation.

Significantly, attitudes toward sexuality and sexual preference are
changing. There is greater acknowledgement that people have different
sexual preferences and diverse sexual practices. Given this reality, it is a
waste of energy for anyone to assume that their condemnation will ensure
that people do not express varied sexual preferences. Many gay people of
all races, raised within this homophobic society, struggle to confront and
accept themselves, to recover or gain the core of self-love and well-being

that is constantly threatened and attacked both from within and without. This is particularly true for people of color who are gay. It is essential that non-gay black people recognize and respect the hardships, the difficulties gay black people experience, extending the love and understanding that is essential for the making of authentic black community. One way we show our care is by vigilant protest of homophobia. By acknowledging the union between black liberation struggle and gay liberation struggle, we strengthen our solidarity, enhance the scope and power of our allegiances, and further our resistance.

18

feminist focus on men: a comment

I

Thinking about men, about masculinity as the subject for a new book I wanted to write, I began to see that in this feminist struggle of ours and in the writings that express the various dimensions of that struggle, there is very little and certainly not enough said about men, about the social construction of masculinity, about the possibilities for transformation. In the early stages of contemporary feminist movement, labeling men "the enemy" or "male chauvinist pigs" was perhaps an effective way for women to begin making the critical separation that would enable rebellion to begin—rebellion against patriarchy, rebellion against male domination. As a strategy of defiance it worked. Men could not consider themselves leaders or even radical participants in feminist movement. Men could not be "feminists." Women were the insiders—men the outsiders. In effect, the women's movement announced its exclusivity. Given this framework, feminist activists and scholars felt little or no responsibility to critically explore the issues of men, to map out feminist strategies for the transformation of masculinity.

As feminist struggle has progressed, as our critical consciousness has deepened and matured, we can see the error in this stance. Now we can acknowledge that the reconstruction and transformation of male behavior, of masculinity, is a necessary and essential part of feminist revolution. Yet critical awareness of the necessity for such work has not led to the production of a significant body of feminist scholarship that fully addresses these issues. Much of the small body of work on men has been done by men.

Only recently have feminist women scholars strongly asserted our concern, our interest in thinking about and doing work on men. Those women who have written about men (for example, Phyllis Chesler and Barbara Ehrenreich) have not talked about their work as though it was in any way exceptional or unique. Given the many feminist works which do not focus in any way on men, it is worthwhile to speculate about and explore the nature of this silence.

For many women, it is not a simple task to talk about men or to consider writing about men. Within patriarchal society, silence has been for women a gesture of submission and complicity, especially silence about men. Women have faithfully kept male secrets, have passionately refused to speak on the subject of men—who they are, how they think, how they behave, how they dominate. This silence is often learned when we are young female children. Many of us were taught that our fathers, because they were men, were not to be spoken to or about, unless they wished to speak with us, and then they were never to be addressed critically.

Growing up in a male-dominated, southern, black, working-class household, we lived as though in two social spaces. One was a world without the father, when he would go to work, and that world was full of speech. Our volumes could be turned up. We could express ourselves loudly, passionately, outrageously. The other world was a male-dominated social space where sound and silence were dictated by his presence. When he returned home (and we would often wait, watch and listen for the sound of him coming), we would adjust our speech to his mood. We would turn our volumes down, lower our voices; we would, if need be, remain silent. In this same childhood world we witnessed women—our grandmothers, mothers, aunts—speak with force and power in sex-segregated spaces, then retreat into a realm of silence in the presence of men. Our grandmother, who talked endlessly, rapidly, harshly, was an example for me and my sisters of the woman we were not to become. Somehow, her mere love of words, of speech, her willingness to fight back, talk back, had stolen male privilege from my grandfather. She had made him less; she had become less. We knew this from listening to what the adults around us said about her and we feared being like her. We feared speech. We feared the words of a woman who could hold her own in any discussion or argument with a man.

Feminist scholarship about women who are physically assaulted by men is full of autobiographical accounts of males punishing women for speaking, whether we speak to defend ourselves, to engage in critical argument, or just to say something—anything. It is as though the very act of speech, wherein a woman talks to a man, carries embedded in that gesture a challenge, a threat to male domination. Perhaps it was a deeply socialized longing to avoid such speech, such confrontation that led contemporary women to promote a feminist activism that devalued the importance of talk with and about men. Perhaps there was a deep-seated fear that we would not emerge from such confrontations triumphant, victorious. Perhaps we feared that feminism would fail us. Certainly many individual feminist women, myself included, have experienced that loss of strength and power as we struggled to talk to and with the men in our lives about male domination, about the need for change. Perhaps a profound despair informed and informs feminist feeling that it is useless to talk to men or about men. Yet to maintain this silence, to not resist it collectively, is to surrender the power that emerges with feminist speech.

In much feminist writing, silence is evoked as a signifier, a marker of exploitation, oppression, dehumanization. Silence is the condition of one who has been dominated, made an object; talk is the mark of freeing, of making one subject. Challenging the oppressed to speak as a way to resist and rebel in *Litany for Survival,* poet Audre Lorde writes:

> and when we speak we are afraid
> our words will not be heard
> nor welcomed
> but when we are silent
> we are still afraid
> So it is better to speak
> remembering
> we were never meant to survive

The act of speaking is a way women come to power, telling our stories, sharing history, engaging in feminist discussion. Early on, feminist consciousness-raising sessions provided a space for women to bear witness to the pain of exploitation and oppression in male-dominated society. Breaking through long silences, many women gave voice for the first time to personal sorrow and anguish, rage, bitterness, and even deep hatred. This speech was a part of women's struggle to resist the silence imposed by male domination. It was an act of resistance. And it was threatening. While it was speech that enabled women to rebel and resist, it was only one stage in the process of feminist education for critical consciousness, one stage in the process of radical transformation.

The next stage would have been the confrontation between women and men, the sharing of this new and radical speech: women speaking to men in a liberated voice. It was this confrontation that has been to a grave extent avoided. Yet it must continually occur if women are to fully enter feminist struggle as subjects and not objects. This confrontational, fundamentally rebellious and defiant feminist speech indicates a change in women's subordinate status. It identifies us as active participants in a revolutionary feminist struggle. In such a struggle, it is essential for the transformation of gender roles, of society that the exploited and oppressed speak to and among ourselves, but it is equally essential that we address without fear those who exploit, oppress, and dominate us. If women remain unable to speak to and about men in a feminist voice then our challenge to male domination on other fronts is seriously undermined.

Sexism is unique. It is unlike other forms of domination—racism or classism—where the exploited and oppressed do not live in large numbers intimately with their oppressors or develop their primary love relationships (familial and/or romantic) with individuals who oppress and dominate or share in the privileges attained by domination. Hence, it is all the more necessary that women speak to men in a liberated voice. The context of these intimate relationships is also the site of domination and oppression. When one girl in four is a victim of male incest, one woman in three is raped, and half of all married women are victims of male violence, addressing ways men and women interact with one another daily must be a concern of feminists. Relationships of care and intimacy often mediate contact between women and men within patriarchy so that all men do not necessarily dominate and oppress women. Despite patriarchy and sexism, there is potential among men for education for critical consciousness, there is possibility for radicalization and transformation. As long as a vast majority of women choose to develop and maintain intimate relationships with men, transformation of these encounters so that they do not become a site for male domination and oppression of women must necessarily be an essential focus of feminist struggle.

Contemporary women's movement in the United States has had great impact on individual women struggling to transform their lives, their particular situations. Not surprisingly, women with the greatest degree of class and race privilege have had the greatest success fighting against the constraints imposed by sexism and domination. Their experience is exceptional. Feminist consciousness-raising for women who do not have these privileges may heighten and intensify frustration and despair rather than serving a liberatory function. It may lead to a greater feeling of powerlessness, hopelessness, and set the stage for debilitating depression. This is particularly the case for those non-privileged women who live in relationships with men, who parent, and who see no way to survive economically or obtain economic self-sufficiency alone. While feminist education for critical consciousness, whether it comes in the form of reading feminist writing or sharing feminist thoughts with a friend, may bring critical self-awareness and greater understanding about the forms male domination takes in their lives, it will not enable them to transform their relationships with men. Feminist works that focus on strategies women can use to speak to males about male domination and change are not readily available, if they exist at all. Yet women have a deep longing to share feminist consciousness with the men in their lives, and together work at transforming their relationships. Concern for this basic struggle should motivate feminist thinkers to talk and write more about how we relate to men and how we change and transform relationships with men characterized by domination.

Considering the extent to which masculinity as it is socially constructed within patriarchy encourages males to regard woman's words, woman's talk as without substance or value, or as a potential threat, individual women cannot hope to effectively communicate feminist thinking with male relatives, companions, etc. without carefully considered strategies. We as women really need to hear from one another about how we communicate feminist thinking to men. Struggling to make a context for dialogue between women and men is a subversive and radical task. Dialogue implies talk between two subjects, not the speech of subject and object. It is a humanizing speech, one that challenges and resists domination.

In *Pedagogy of the Oppressed*, Paulo Freire emphasizes the importance of dialogue and connects it to the struggle of the oppressed to become subjects. He stresses that, "Love is at the same time the foundation of dialogue and dialogical itself. It is thus necessarily the task of responsible Subjects and cannot exist in a relation of domination." Freire comments further, "I am more and more convinced that true revolutionaries must perceive the revolution, because of its creative and liberating nature, as an act of love... The distortion imposed on the word *love* by the capitalist world cannot prevent the revolution from being essentially loving in character..." Significantly, male domination suppresses this dialogue that is essential to love, so that women and men cannot hear themselves talking to one another as they go about their daily lives. As feminists speak more to women and men about patriarchy, it is important that we address the truth that circumstances of male domination make authentic, loving relationships between most women and men impossible. We must distinguish between the bonds of care and commitment that develop in a dominant-submissive, subject-object encounter and that care and commitment which emerges in a context of non-domination, of reciprocity, of mutuality. It is this bonding that enables sustained love, that enables men and women to nurture one another, to grow fully and freely.

Male domination has not destroyed the longing men and women have to love one another, even though it makes fulfilling that longing almost impossible to realize. The context of love between males and females is varied and multidimensional (there is the relationship between mother and son, sister and brother, father and daughter, etc.). Whenever this longing to love exists there is present the possibility that the forms of discourse within patriarchy that estrange and alienate women and men from one another can be resisted, that a context for dialogue can be created, that a liberatory exchange can take place. However, dialogue can only emerge if there is awareness that women and men must consciously alter the way we talk to and about one another so that we do not perpetuate and reinforce male domination. Failure to focus on the ways women and men talk to one another or refusal to address this problem because it means we must speak about and/or to men significantly retard feminist movement. Most women active in feminist struggle—whether it be the efforts of a lesbian daughter to communicate with a father, or the effort wife and husband make, or the efforts of friends—have had to confront males as we try to share feminist thinking. To know the strategies that have made dialogues possible, that have made for reconciliation and communication, would be useful information to share. It will not be shared as long as feminist activists do not assert the primacy of work by women about men.

Many feminist women who teach, who do feminist scholarship have engaged in difficult and often bitter struggles to make a space for dialogue with males in our private and work lives. In these confrontations, we have learned more effective ways to communicate feminist thinking with men. Many of us have tried to make a space for dialogue in our classrooms. When Women's Studies and feminist classrooms were primarily peopled by young women eager to learn and share feminist perspectives, willing to commit themselves to feminist struggle, we were not compelled to develop strategies that would make communication with male students possible. It has been the growing presence of men in my classrooms that has led me to consider both the difficulties that arise when we work to communicate feminist thinking to men and the importance of such communication. This experience has also compelled me to recognize the need for more scholarship by women about men.

Just as love relationships between females and males are a space where feminist struggle to make a context for dialogue can take place, feminist teaching and scholarship can also and must necessarily be a space for dialogue. It is in that space that we share feminist thinking with a willing audience. It is in that space that we can engage in constructive confrontation and critique. Stereotypes that feminist women are man-hating cause many teachers to feel awkward when making critical comments about men, especially when there is the recognition that more and more males need to engage in feminist struggle if there is to be an end to sexist oppression, to male domination. Not wanting to reinforce the stereotype, feminist women professors are often reluctant to discuss masculinity critically, or the ways in which sexism seriously limits men, or we raise these issues in ways that alienate, that convey ridicule, contempt, or our own uncertainty. Feminist scholars must be a vanguard, mapping out a terrain where women can speak to and about men in ways that challenge but do not diminish.

Challenging and changing the way feminist women scholars talk to and about men and promoting more work on men is an important direction for revolutionary feminist struggle. While it is critical that male scholars committed to feminist struggle do scholarship that focusses on men, it is equally important that women scholars focus on men. When women scholars write about men, such work alters the subject-object relationship that has been a sign of our exploited and oppressed state. Our perspective can provide unique and critical insight, as well as connecting us intimately with the day-to-day struggle of all women who are seeking to make a space for dialogue with men, a space that is not shaped by domination. Rather than focussing on men in a way that renders them objects, feminist scholarship on men by women is informed by a politic that resists domination, that is humanizing and liberatory. This feminist scholarship is informed by the longing for a subject-to-subject encounter, by the longing for a meeting place, a place for solidarity where women can speak to and/or about men in a feminist voice, where our words can be heard, where we can speak the truth that heals, that transforms—that makes feminist revolution.

19

"whose pussy is this":
a feminist comment

Before I see Spike Lee's film, *She's Gotta Have It*, I hear about it. Folks tell me "it's black, it's funny, it's something you don't want to miss." With all this talk, especially coming from black folks who don't usually go to the movies, I become reluctant, even suspicious. If everybody is liking it, even white folks, something has got to be wrong somewhere! Initially, these are the thoughts that keep me from seeing the film but I don't stay away long. When I receive letters and phone calls from black women scholars and friends telling me about the film and wanting to talk about whether it portrays a liberated black woman, I make my way to the movies. I don't go alone. I go with black women friends Beverly, Yvette, and Maria so we can talk about it together. Some of what was said that evening in the heat of our discussion informs my comments.

A passionate viewer of films, especially the work of independent filmmakers, I found much to appreciate in the technique, style, and over-all production of *She's Gotta Have It*. It was especially refreshing to see images of black people on screen that were not grotesque caricatures, images that were familiar, images that imaginatively captured the essence, dignity, and spirit of that elusive quality know as "soul." It was a very soulful film.

Thinking about the film from a feminist perspective, considering its political implications, I find it much more problematic. In the article, "Art vs. Ideology: The Debate Over Positive Images" (*Black Film Review*, Vol.

2, No. 3), Salim Muwakkil raises the question of whether a "mature African-American community" can allow "aesthetic judgments to rest on ideological or political criteria," commenting:

> The black cultural nationalists of the 60s and 70s demonstrated anew the deadening effect such ideological requirements have on creative expression. Their various proscriptions and prescriptions aborted a historical moment pregnant with promise. It seems clear that efforts to subordinate the profound and penetrating creative process of black people to an ideological movement suffocates the community's creative vitality.

While I would emphatically assert that aesthetic judgments should not rest *solely* on ideological or political criteria, this does not mean that such criteria cannot be used in conjunction with other critical strategies to assess the overall value of a given work. It does not imply a devaluation to engage in critical discussion of those criteria. To deny the validity of an aesthetic critique that encompasses the ideological or political is to mask the truth that every aesthetic work embodies the political, the ideological as part of its fundamental structure. No aesthetic work transcends politics or ideology.

Significantly, the film *She's Gotta Have It* was advertised, marketed, and talked about in reviews and conversations in a manner that raised political and ideological questions both about the film and the public responses to it. Was the film "a woman's story"? Did the film depict a radically new image of black female sexuality? Can a man really tell a woman's story? One viewer posed the question to me as: "Is Nola Darling a liberated woman or just a WHORE." (This is the way this sentence was written in a letter to me by a black woman professor who teaches film, who wrote that she was "waiting for the feminist response.") There has been no widespread feminist response to the film precisely because of the overwhelming public celebration of that which is new, different, and exciting in this work. Given the pervasive anti-feminism in popular culture, in black subculture, a feminist critique might simply be aggressively dismissed. Yet for feminist thinkers to avoid public critique is to diminish the power of the film. It is a testimony to that power that it compels us to think, to reflect, to engage the work fully.

Recently, the film version of Alice Walker's *The Color Purple* evoked more discussion among black folks of feminist issues (sexism, freedom of sexual expression, male violence against women, etc.) than any theoretical and/or polemical work by feminist scholars. *She's Gotta Have It* generated a similar response. Often these discussions exposed grave ignorance about feminist political movement, revealing the extent to which shallow notions of feminist struggle disseminated by non-feminists in popular culture shape and influence the way many black people perceive feminism. That all feminists are man-hating, sexually depraved, castrating, power-hungry, etc. are prevailing stereotypes. The tendency to see liberated women as sexually loose informed the way many people viewed the portrayal of black female sexuality in *She's Gotta Have It*. To some extent, this perception is based on a narrowly defined notion of liberation that was acceptable in some feminist circles at one time.

During the early stages of contemporary women's movement, feminist liberation was often equated with sexual liberation by both feminist activists and non-feminists. At that time, the conceptualization of female sexual liberation was informed by a fierce heterosexist bias which saw sexual liberation primarily in terms of women asserting the right to be sexually desiring, to initiate sexual relationships, and to participate in casual sexual encounters with varied male partners. Women dared to assert that female sexuality was not passive, that women were desiring subjects who both longed for and enjoyed sex as much if not more than men. These assertions could have easily provided the ideological framework for the construction of a character like Nola Darling, the main female character in *She's Gotta Have It*. Nola expressed again and again her eagerness and willingness to be sexual with men as well as her right to have numerous partners.

Superficially, Nola Darling is the perfect embodiment of woman as desiring subject—a representation which does challenge sexist notions of female sexual passivity. (It is important to remember that from slavery on, black women have been portrayed in white racist thought as sexually assertive although this view contrasts sharply with the emphasis on chastity, monogamy, and male right to initiate sexual contact in black culture, a view held especially among the middle classes.) Ironically and unfortunately, Nola Darling's sexual desire is not depicted as an autonomous gesture, as an independent longing for sexual expression, satisfaction, and fulfillment. Instead her assertive sexuality is most often portrayed as though her body, her sexually aroused being is a reward or gift she bestows on the deserving male. When body builder Greer Childs tells Nola that his photo will appear on the cover of a popular men's magazine, she responds by removing her clothes, by offering her body as a token of her esteem. This and other incidents suggest that Nola, though desiring subject, acts on the assumption that heterosexual female sexual assertion has legitimacy primarily as a gesture of reward or as a means by which men can be manipulated and controlled by women (what is vulgarly called "pussy power"). Men do not have to objectify Nola's sexuality because she objectifies it. In so doing, her character becomes the projection of a stereotypical sexist notion of a sexually assertive woman—she is not in fact liberated.

While Nola is not passive sexually, her primary concern is pleasing each partner. Though we are led to believe she enjoys sex, her sexual fulfillment is never the central concern. She is pleasured only to the extent that she is able to please. While her partners enjoy being sexual with her, they are disturbed by her desire to have frequent sex with several partners.

They see her sexual longing as abnormal. One male partner, Mars, says, "all men want freaks (in bed), we just don't want 'em for a wife." This comment illustrates the sexist stereotypes about female sexuality that inform Mars' perceptions of Nola. When Jaime, another partner, suggests that Nola is sick, evoking sexist stereotypes to label her insane, depraved, abnormal, Nola does not respond by asserting that she is sexually liberated. Instead she internalizes the critique and seeks psychiatric help. Throughout the film, she is extremely dependent on male perceptions of her reality. Lacking self-awareness and the capacity to be self-critical, she explores her sexuality only when compelled to do so by a man. If Nola were sexually liberated, there would be no need for her to justify or defend herself against male accusations. It is only after the men have passed judgement that she begins the process of coming to consciousness. Until that point, we know more about how the men in the film see her than how she sees herself.

To a very grave extent the focus of the film is not Nola but her male partners. Just as they are the center of attention sexually, they are also central personalities in the film. In telling us what they think about Nola, they tell us more about themselves, their values, their desires. She is the object that stimulates the discourse, they are its subjects. The narrators are male and the story is a male-centered, male-biased patriarchal tale. As such, it is not progressive nor does it break away from the traditional portrayal of female sexuality in film. *She's Gotta Have It* can take its place alongside a growing body of contemporary films that claim to tell women's stories while privileging male narratives, films that stimulate audiences with versions of female sexuality that are not really new or different (*Paris, Texas* for example). Another recently acclaimed film, *Mona Lisa,* objectifies black womanhood and black female sexuality in a similar way.

Overall, it is the men who speak in *She's Gotta Have It.* While Nola appears one-dimensional in perspective and focus, seemingly more concerned about her sexual relationships than about any other aspect of her life, the male characters are multi-dimensional. They have personalities. Nola has no personality. She is shallow, vacuous, empty. Her one claim to fame is that she likes to fuck. In the male pornographic imagination she could be described as "pure pussy," that is to say that her ability to perform sexually is the central, defining aspect of her identity.

These sexually active, sexually hungry men are not "pure penis" because there is no such category. They are each defined by unique characteristics and attributes—Mars by his humor, Greer by his obsession with body building, Jaime by his concern with romance and committed relationships. Unlike Nola, they are not always thinking about sex, do not suffer from penis on the brain. They have opinions on a variety of topics: politics, sports, lifestyles, gender, etc. Filmmaker Spike Lee challenges and critiques notions of black male sexuality while presenting a very typical perspective on black female sexuality. His imaginative explorations of black male psyche is far more probing, far more expansive, and finally much more interesting than his exploration of black femaleness.

When Nola testifies that there have been "dogs" in her life—men who were only concerned with getting into bed—a group of black men appear on the screen in single file delivering the lines they use to seduce women, to "get it." In this brief segment, sexist male objectification of females is exposed along with the falseness and superficiality of the men. This particular scene, more than any other in the film, is an excellent example of how cinema can be effectively used to raise consciousness about political concerns—in this case sexist male objectification of females. Without any particular character making a heavy-handed statement about how shallowly these black men think about women and sexuality, this point is powerfully conveyed. Filmmaker Spike Lee acknowledges that he intended to focus critically on black male behavior in the film stating, "I know that black men do a lot of things that are fucked up, and I've tried to show some of the things that we do."

While his innovative portrayal of black men in this scene (which is shot in such a way as to assume a documentary stance—each man appearing in single file before a camera as though they are being individually interviewed—acts to expose and, by implication, critique black male sexism, other scenes reinforce and perpetuate it. The deconstructive power of this scene is undermined most glaringly by the rape scene which occurs later.

Often talking with folks about the movie, I found many people did not notice that there was a rape scene, while others questioned whether it could be accurately described as a rape. Those of us who understand rape to be an act of coercive sexual contact, wherein one person is forced by another to participate without consent, watched a rape scene in *She's Gotta Have It*. When I first saw the film with the black women friends mentioned earlier, we were surprised and disturbed by the rape scene, yet we did not yell out in protest or leave the theater. As a group, we collectively sunk in our seats as though hiding. It was not the imaginative portrayal of rape that was shocking and disturbing, but the manner and style of this depiction. In this instance, rape as an act of black male violence against a black woman was portrayed as though it was just another enjoyable sexual encounter, just another fuck. Rape, the film implies, is a difficult term to use when describing forced sexual intercourse with a sexually active female (in this case it is called a "near rape"). After all, as many black folks—women and men—stressed in conversation with me, "she called him—she wanted to be sexual—she wanted it." Embedded in such thinking is the sexist assumption that woman as desiring subject, as active initiator, as sexual seducer is responsible for the quality, nature, and content of male response.

Not surprisingly, Nola sees herself as accountable, yet her ability to judge situations clearly has been questioned throughout the film. While she is completely in character when she labels the rape a "near rape," the fact remains that she is raped. Though she is depicted as deriving pleasure from the act, this does not alter the fact that she is forced to act sexually without her consent. It is perfectly compatible with sexist pornographic fantasies about rape to show a woman enjoying violation. Since the sexist mindset places responsibility on the female, claiming that she is really in control, then such a fantasy allows that she (who is in actuality a victim) has the power to change this violent act into a pleasurable experience.

Hence the look on Darling's face during the rape which begins as a grimace reflecting pain ends as a gaze of pleasure, satisfaction. This is most assuredly a sexist imaginative fantasy of rape—one that we as passive, silent viewers condone by our complicity. Protests from the audience would have at least altered passive acceptance of this depiction of rape. In keeping with the reality of patriarchy, with sexism in our culture, viewers who were pleased with the rape cheered and expressed their approval of Jaime's action when I saw the film.

As Jaime rapes Nola and aggressively demands that she answer the question, "whose pussy is this," this is the moment of truth—the moment when she can declare herself independent, sexually liberated, the moment when she can proudly assert through resistance her sexual autonomy (for the film has highlighted her determination to be sexually active, to choose many partners, to belong to no one). Ironically, she does not resist the physical violence. She does not assert the primacy of her body rights. She is passive. It is ironic because until this moment we have been seduced by the image of her as a forceful woman, a woman who dares to be sexually assertive, demanding, active. We are seduced and betrayed. When Nola responds to the question,"whose pussy is this" by saying "yours," it is difficult for anyone who has fallen for the image of her as sexually liberated not to feel let down, disappointed both in her character and in the film. Suddenly we are not witnessing a radical questioning of female sexual passivity or a celebration of female sexual self-assertion but a reconstruction of the same old sexist content in a new and more interesting form. While some of us were passively disgusted, disturbed, sexist male viewers feeling villified cheered, expressing their satisfaction that the uppity black woman had been put in her place—that male domination and patriarchal order were restored.

After the rape, Nola ceases to be sexually active, chooses to be in a monogamous relationship with Jaime, the partner who has coerced her. Ideologically, such a scenario impresses on the consciousness of black males, and all males, the sexist assumption that rape is an effective means of patriarchal social control, that it restores and maintains male power over women. It simultaneously suggests to black females, and all females, that being sexually assertive will lead to rejection and punishment. In a culture where a woman is raped every eighteen seconds, where there is still enormous ignorance about rape, where patriarchy and sexist practices promote and condone rape of women by men as a way to maintain male domination, it is disturbing to witness this scene not only because it reinforces dangerous stereotypes (a central one being that women enjoy rape), but because it suggests that rape does not have severe and grave consequences for victims. Without counseling, without support, Nola is restored to her cool, confident self by the end of the movie. Silent about her sexuality throughout much of the film, she suddenly speaks. It is she who will call the rape a "near rape," as though it was really no big deal.

Yet it is the rape that shifts the direction of the film, of Nola Darling's fictional self-exploration. As an expression of her newly acquired self-assertion, she calmly denounces the "near rape," explains that the relationship with Jaime has not worked, while stressing her right to be autonomously self-defining. Expressed without the bravado and zest that has characterized her previous actions, these statements do not dispel the pervasive sense that we have witnessed a woman being disempowered and not a woman coming to power. This seems to be reconfirmed when Nola's choice to be truly self-defining means that she will be alone, with no sexual partner.

In perfect contrast to *The Color Purple*, wherein same-sex relationships between women are depicted as a source of mutual, non-exploitative erotic affirmation that serve as catalysts for self-development, the lesbian sexuality in *She's Gotta Have It* is negatively portrayed. It does not represent an alternative to destructive heterosexual practice. The lesbian character is predatory, as much a "dog" as any of the men. Significantly, Nola does not find it difficult to reject unwanted sexual advances from another woman, to assert her body rights, her preferences. Utterly male-identified, she does not value her women friends. Though they are underdeveloped characters in the film, her two female friends are compelling and interesting. The apparent dedication and discipline the bass player shows in relationship to her music stands in sharp contrast to Nola's lackadaisical approach to her art, whereas the bass player appears comfortable with her autonomy in a way that Nola is not.

Autonomy is not depicted as a life-enhancing, empowering choice for Nola. Her decision to be self-defining leaves her as vacuous and as empty as she has previously appeared without the savvy she had evoked in her role as vamp. Finally we see her at the end of the film alone, wrapped in her sheets, a familiar image that does not suggest transformation. Are we to imagine that she has ceased to long for the "it" she's gotta have? Are we to think that the "it" is multiple in implication after all, that it may not be sex but a sense of self she is longing for? She has had sex throughout the film; what she has not had is a sense of self that would enable her to be fully autonomous and sexually assertive, independent, and liberated. Without a firm sense of self her attempts at becoming a desiring subject rather than object are doomed to fail. Nola cannot enter the sexual power struggle between women and men as object and become subject. Desire alone is not enough to make her subject, to liberate (the film does make this point, but this is no new revelation). A new image, the one we have yet to see in film is the desiring black woman who prevails, who triumphs, not desexualized, not alone, who is "together" in every sense of the word. Joan Mellen in her introduction to *Women and Their Sexuality in the New Film* emphasizes that the recent attempt to portray radical and transformative images of female sexuality has proved to be a disappointment, in most instances a failure:

> The language of independent women may be reluctantly allowed, but the substance goes unaltered. If lip service provides a pseudo-anticipation of challenge to old values and images, the real business at hand is to refurbish the established view, now strengthened by nominal reference to "awareness." This sleight of hand is the method of co-option. Cinema is an arena in which the process had been refined. Thus the very image of liberated or self-sufficient women, when it is risked on the screen, is presented unpalatably and deployed to reinforce the old ways.

Even though filmmaker Spike Lee may have intended to portray a radical new image of black female sexuality, *She's Gotta Have It* reinforces and perpetuates old norms overall. Positively, the film does show us the nature of black male/female power struggles, the contradictions, the craziness, and that is an important new direction. Yet it is the absence of compelling liberatory reconciliation which undermines the progressive radical potential of this film. Even though nude scenes, scenes of sexual play constitute an important imaging of black sexuality on screen since they are not grotesque or pornographic, we still do not see an imaging of mutual, sexually satisfying relationships between black women and men in a context of non-domination. It does not really matter if the woman is dominating and a male submitting—it is the same old oppressive scenario. Ultimately it is a patriarchal tale—one in which woman does not emerge triumphant, fulfilled. While we can applaud Nola's feeble attempt to tell a new story at the end of the film, it is not compelling, not enough—it is not satisfying.

20

black women writing: creating more space

To many people, black women writers are everywhere—on the cover of *Newsweek*, the *New York Times Magazine*, on talk shows, on speaking circuits. Just the other day I was in a bookstore and the clerk who took my money for Paule Marshall's novel *Praisesong For The Widow* told me if I intend to write a novel, this is the time—that "they" are looking for black women writers. "They" are the publishers and they are supposedly looking for us because our work is a new commodity. The invisible "they" who control publishing may have only recently fully realized that there is a market for fiction written by black women, but it does not necessarily follow that they are actively seeking to find more material by black women; that black women are writing more than ever before; or that it is any easier for unknown black women writers to find ways to publish their work. It is more likely that those black women writers who have been writing unnoticed for some time, who have already found a way to get their foot in the door or have managed to open it wider, have managed to enter and can now find publishers for their work. Publication of their work reminds me and many black women writers/readers that our voices can be heard, that if we create, there is "hope" that our work will one day be published. I am always excited when I hear that another black woman writer has published (fiction or any other genre), especially if she is new and unknown. The more of us there are entering the publishing world the more likely we will continue writing. Yet we are not entering the publishing world in large numbers. Every time someone comments on the "tremendous" attention black women writers are receiving, how easy it is for us to find publishers, how many of us there are, I stop and count, make lists, sit in groups of black women and try to come up with new names. What we've noticed is that the number of visible published black women writers of fiction is not large. Anyone who teaches courses on black women's fiction knows how difficult it is to find the works of black women (they go out of print rapidly, do not get reprinted, or if reprinted come out in editions that are so expensive that students and part-time lecturers like myself can rarely afford to buy them for their personal libraries and certainly cannot teach them in classes where many books must be purchased). The reprinted edition of Gwendolyn Brooks' *Maud Martha* (first published in 1953) is one example. It is, however, better to have expensive reprints rather than no reprints. Books like Ann Petry's *The Street*, Jessie Fausett's *Plum Bun*, Frances Harper's *Iola Leroy*, Kristin Hunter's *The Survivors* and *The Lakestown Rebellion* are not always available. Yet all of these black women writers were or are well-known and their works were or are widely read.

I assume that publishing quotas exist that determine the number of black women who will publish books of fiction yearly. Such quotas are not consciously negotiated and decided upon but are the outcomes of institutionalized racism, sexism, and classism. These systems of domination operate in such a way as to ensure that only a very few fiction books by black women will be published at any given time. This has many negative implications for black women writers, those who are published and those who have yet to be published. Published black women writers, even those who are famous, are well aware that their successes do not ensure that their books will be on bookstore shelves years from now. They know that the spirit of new commodity fadism that stimulates much of the current interest in black women's writing can dissipate. It is likely that these writers know that they must "strike while the iron is hot" and this knowledge produces the sense that they cannot always wait for inspiration, cannot linger too long between the publication of one book and the writing of another. They are often compelled to spread themselves thin—teaching, writing, giving talks in the interest of making a living but also in the interest of promoting awareness of the existence and significance of their work. These pressures, whether imposed or chosen, will necessarily affect the writer's work.

Black women writers who are not published, who are still nourishing and developing their skills often find it difficult to maintain the sense that what they have to say is important, especially if they are not in an environment where their commitment to writing is encouraged and affirmed. They must also struggle with the demands of surviving economically while writing. The difficulty of this process for black women has changed little through the years. For every one black woman writer that manages to be published, hundreds if not thousands cease writing because they cannot withstand the pressures, cannot sustain the effort without affirmation, or because they fear that to risk everything in pursuit of one's creative work seems foolish because so few will make it in the end.

Often new writers find that college creative writing courses provide a positive atmosphere wherein one's work will be read, critiqued, affirmed. Black women attending universities could and do find in such courses a place to strengthen creative writing skills. However, black students are rarely present in these courses at campuses where students are predominantly white. At some campuses where students are predominantly black there is often little or no interest in creative writing. Young black women recognize the precariousness of our collective economic lot (increased unemployment, poverty, etc.) and tend to look for those courses that strengthen their ability to succeed in careers. The promising young black woman writer who must work to provide or help provide for herself and family often cannot find the energy or time to concentrate on and develop her writing. Often black women in professions (teachers, doctors, lawyers, etc.) who are also writers find that the demands of their jobs leave little room for the cultivation of creative work.

Few black women have imagined that they can make a living writing. I was thirteen when I decided that I wanted to be a writer. At that time I was primarily writing poetry and I realized that I would not be able to make a living with writing. I chose to study literature because I thought it would lead to a profession compatible with writing. When poetry was my primary concern I was fascinated by the work lives of poets who had professions but wrote extensively. Many of these poets were men—Langston Hughes, Wallace Stevens, William Carlos Williams. When I read about their lives I did not reflect on the supportive role women played in the lives of heterosexual male writers, who were probably not coping with domestic chores or raising children while working in professional jobs and writing (their female companions probably attended to these matters). Rare is the woman writer of any race who is free (from domestic chores or caring for others—children, parents, companions) to focus solely on her writing. I know of few black women writers who have been able to concentrate solely on their development as writers without working other jobs at the same time.

In retrospect, I can see that I was always trying to attend college, hold part-time jobs, and make a space for writing, as well as take care of domestic matters. It has become clear to me that I was most free to develop as a writer/poet when I was home with my parents and they were providing economic support, with mama doing the majority of domestic chores and all the cooking. This was the time in my life when I had time to read, study, and write. They and my siblings were also continually affirming my creativity, urging me to develop my talent (after I did my small number of assigned chores). I often heard from them and other folk in the community that talent was a gift from God and was not to be taken lightly but nourished, developed, or it would be taken away. While I no longer hear this message literally—that the ability to write will be taken away—I do see that the more I write the easier and more joyous a labor it becomes. The less I write the harder it is for me to write and the more it appears to be so arduous a task that I seek to avoid it. I think if any would-be-writer avoids writing long enough then they are likely to "lose" the desire—the ability—the power to create.

One must write and one must have time to write. Having time to write, time to wait through silences, time to go to the pen and paper or typewriter when the breakthrough finally comes, affects the type of work that is written. When I read contemporary black women's fiction I see much similarity in choices of subject matter, geographical location, use of language, character formation and style. There could be many reasons for such similarities. On the one hand, there is the reality of the social status black women share which has been shaped by the impact of sexism and racism on our lives and shared cultural and ethnic experiences. On the other hand, there is the possibility that many of us pattern work after the fiction of those writers who have been published and are able to earn a living as writers. There is also the possibility that a certain type of writing (the linear narrative story) may be easier to write because it is more acceptable to the reading public than experimental works, especially those that would not focus on themes of black experience or tell a story in a more conventional way. These restrictions apply to many groups of writers in our society. It is important that there be diversity in the types of fictions black women produce and that varied types of writing by black women receive attention and be published. There should not be a stereotyped image of a black woman writer or a preconceived assumption about the type of fiction she will produce.

It must not be assumed that the successes of contemporary black women writers like Toni Morrison, Alice Walker, Paule Marshall, Toni Cade Bambara, Ntozake Shange and others indicate that a new day has arrived for a majority or even a substantial minority of black women writers. Their individual successes and continued creative development are crucial components of what should be an overall artistic movement to encourage and support writing by black women. Such a movement could take many forms. On a very basic level it can begin with communities stressing the importance of young black children acquiring reading and writing skills and developing along with those skills a positive attitude toward writing. Many of us learned reading and writing but disliked or hated writing. Throughout my six years of part-time teaching at a number of universities, I have witnessed the terror and anguish many students feel about writing. Many acknowledge that their hatred and fear of writing surfaced in grade school and gathered momentum through high school reaching a paralyzing peak in the college years.

An intense effort to create and sustain interest in writing must take place in schools and communities. Entering writing competitions should be encouraged by parents, teachers, and friends for young writers. Black women and other people who are interested in the future development of black writers should establish more writing competitions where prizes could be as low as $25 to stimulate interest in writing. There should be grant programs for newly published but not yet successful black women writers so that we can have a summer or a year to concentrate solely on our work. Though programs exist that fund writers (like the National Endowment for the Humanities), only the occasional lucky black woman writer receives one of these grants. Often the same few writers receive a number of grants from different sources. While this is good for the individual, it does not increase the number of black women writers receiving aid. Money could be given to a number of universities to sponsor black women as part of creative writing programs.

It seems easier for black women writers to receive monetary support of one kind or another, grants, teaching positions and talks after they have struggled in isolation and achieved success. Yet only a few black women writers make it in this way. It took me seven years to finish the writing of *Ain't I A Woman: Black Women and Feminism* in part because I did extensive research before writing but also because every avenue I turned toward seeking monetary support failed. I would write after working my eight hours a day at the phone company or after other jobs. When the book was completed almost three years before it was published, I sent it off to a number of publishers who rejected it. Although I always asked editors for feedback as to why the work was not acceptable/accepted, I never received any answer. Without the support of my companion, who helped both financially and emotionally (affirming me as a writer), it would have been impossible to continue. I hear this same story from other black women who know firsthand, as I do, how devastating working in isolation can be. On several occasions I contacted established black women writers seeking acceptance, advice and critiques but got little response. However, Alice Walker was one person who told me that she was very busy but would take time to read the manuscript if she could. I did not send it to her because I felt that I was imposing, perhaps taking her attention away from her work. Also I think the other black women writers I approached were constantly asked to respond, to give support and advice to younger writers and there is a point when one must say no if one is overextended.

Black women need not be the only group who give support and affirmation to aspiring black female writers. A teacher, friend, or colleague can provide the encouragement and affirmation that fosters and promotes work. When I first met recently published black woman writer Gloria Naylor, author of the novel *The Women of Brewster Place*, I asked her how she had found a publisher. Gloria was a student at Yale working on an M.A. focussing on creative writing. She found support and affirmation for her work in this academic environment. It was with the help of a friend that she was able to find an editor to read her novel and consider it for publication. Having people around who affirm one during the writing process is as vital to the aspiring writer as finding someone to publish one's work.

When I was an undergraduate taking creative writing courses, I remember a black male poet advising me not to worry about publication but to focus on writing, then when I had produced a body of work to worry about finding a publisher. This bit of advice has been very useful over the years reminding me that the primary emphasis for the aspiring writer has to be initially on the production of work. I find in teaching creative writing classes that aspiring writers are often so desperate for the affirmation that comes with publication that they are not interested in rewriting, or putting away a piece for a time and coming back to it. After *Ain't I A Woman* was rejected I spent almost nine months away from the work before I took the box down from its hiding place in the closet and began massive rewriting. Like Gloria Naylor, I learned that South End Press was seeking books on feminism and race from a friend who had seen their ad in a Bay area women's newspaper. In retrospect, despite the pain I suffered when the manuscript was continually rejected, I can see now that it was not ready for publication at that time. I now consider it fortunate that no one accepted it then. I have completed two books that focus on feminist issues, one poetry manuscript, one dissertation, two novels in manuscript, and yet I still confront daily the difficulty of providing for myself economically while seeking to grow and develop as a writer.

When I told Chinosole, a black woman friend and fellow writer-scholar, about this essay, she commented that it is amazing how much writing we black women can produce even when we are worried sick about finances and job pressures. It is my hope that the current interest in the works of a few black women writers will lead to the recognition of the need to encourage and promote such writing—not just the work of famous black women but the work of unknown, struggling, aspiring writers who need to know that their creative work is important, that it deserves their concentrated attention, and that it need not be abandoned.

21

Ain't I A Woman: *looking back*

This essay was written shortly after the publication of *Ain't I A Woman: Black Women and Feminism*. Now I cannot even remember the context for which I wrote. On reading it, I was surprised by the many sentences which begin with the word "I." The text seemed raw and awkward. I considered not including it in this book, or writing a more updated version, then I decided to let this voice speak even though I might not make the same statements in quite the same way at this moment.

I cannot recall when I first heard the word "feminist" or understood its meaning. I know that it was early childhood that I began to wonder about sex roles, that I began to see and feel that the experience of being "made" female was different from that of being "made" male; perhaps I was so conscious of this because my brother was my constant companion. I use the word "made" because it was obvious in our home that sex roles were socially constructed—that everyone could agree that very small children were pretty much alike, only different from one another physiologically; but that everyone enjoyed the process of turning us into little girls and little boys, little men and little women, with socially constructed differences. As a little girl without sex role expectations, I could follow my father down to Virginia Street. In those days Virginia Street was a black male world with barber shops, pool halls, liquor stores, and pawn shops. My father and sometimes my uncles took me there, shared with me the intimacy of this world of black male bonding and kinship. When I

148

began to grow up, my mother decided these trips had to stop—Virginia Street was no place for a nice little girl. I've been told that I cried bitterly when I was no longer allowed to go there.

By my teenage years, I had learned this lesson well. I feared the world of Virginia Street. I no longer felt the intimate sweet companionship with strange black males and even the old familiar faces. They were the enemies of one's virginity. They had the power to transform woman's reality—to turn her from a good woman into a bad woman, to make her a whore, a slut. Even "good" women suffered, were somehow always at the mercy of men, who could judge us unfit, unworthy of love, kindness, tenderness, who could, if they chose to do so, destroy us. It was in the world of that street and our segregated black community that I first saw men actively suppressing the growth of women, and in that world that I saw women resisting, taking risks—striving. It was in that world that I learned about male violence against women, black women dying in childbirth, about the sexual harassment of black women on jobs, about the necessity of staying away from white men because they could rape us with impunity. It was in that world that I told mama, "I don't think I'll ever marry, seems like women just lose something in marriage." It was in that world that my father, with the agreement of my mother, sought to deny me the right to attend Stanford University because it was too far away for a country girl to go by herself. I accepted this decision initially and then rebelled.

These experiences forged and tempered my feminist spirit and I eagerly responded to the fervor over contemporary feminist movement on campus. I took classes, went to meetings, to all-women's parties. It was in one of my first Women's Studies classes, taught by Tillie Olsen, that I noticed the complete absence of material by or any discussion about black women. I began to feel estranged and alienated from the huge group of white women who were celebrating the power of "sisterhood." I could not understand why they did not notice "absences" or care. When I confronted our teacher, she expressed regret and began to cry. I was not moved. I did not want sympathy, I wanted action. I was alone in that class of white women who did not even begin to understand my feelings or care about them, all they knew was that I was spoiling their celebration, their "sisterhood," their "togetherness." Contrary to what many people think, critiques about the absence of material on black women in such classes do not emerge because black women are eager to call white women on their racism, put them down, or make them feel bad, but because we go to these classes hoping to gain knowledge, to strengthen our awareness of our history—our struggles. These are the same reasons many white students come to Women's Studies classes, only they are not disappointed by absences, by no focus on their reality. They do not walk out of such classes into a void where they are still invisible, their history unknown, their reality denied.

Attending such classes, I reached a very real point of desperation and urgency; I needed to know about black woman's reality. I needed even to understand this feeling of difference and separation from white women peers. I knew from gut level, everyday life experience that to be a black woman in this culture was to have a social reality that differed from that of white men, white women, and even black men, but I did not know how to explain this difference. I did not know enough about black women's history. When I began the long search in history, sociology, and psychology texts for material, I was really surprised and even shocked that black women were rarely a category in anyone's index, that when we were written about we rarely rated more than a few sentences or paragraphs. (I did not know then of the great wealth of material to be found by and about black women in dissertations, especially those of students from predominantly black colleges.) Although I searched in primary and secondary sources, I could not find material that made connections between racism and sexism or research on black people that fully considered gender differences.

In retrospect, I can see that much of my disappointment, my sense of urgency had to do with the fear that the absence of material about black women was linked to the absence of a model of liberation that would free us from the tyranny of both racism and sexism. I had already begun to question and examine ways in which sexism and racism worked together to ensure the oppression and exploitation of black women yet I wanted to learn from other sources. During this period of desperation and urgency, I continually complained to the black companion I lived with about the dearth of material. When I could not find sources, when I expressed mounting bitterness and rage, he encouraged me to write this book that I was searching for. His suggestion is one I often refer to both to dispel the notion that "all" black men oppose and suppress black women's interest in critically reflecting about gender and resisting sexism and to point to the reality that, at that time, I would not have imagined myself as a writer creating such a book. At age nineteen, coming from a small Kentucky town, I did not think of myself as having the power to define my social reality, to give voice in written form to my thoughts on black female experience of sexism. These self-perceptions were informed by racism and sexism.

My longing to find sources that would explain black female experience (especially my assumption that books written by white people would contain such information) is precisely a reflection of the socialization of oppressed and exploited groups in a culture of domination. We learn that we do not have the power to define our own reality or to transform oppressive structures. We learn to look to those empowered by the very systems of domination that wound and hurt us for some understanding of who we are that will be liberating and we never find that. It is necessary for us to do the work ourselves if we want to know more about our experience, if we want to see that experience from perspectives not shaped by domination.

Ain't I A Woman: Black Women and Feminism did not emerge from any desire on my part to explain black women to white feminist women or to capitalize on an interest in racial issues. At that time, race was not a popular topic among feminists. The book emerged out of my longing for self-recovery, for education for critical consciousness—for a way of understanding black female experience that would liberate us from the colonizing mentality fostered in a racist, sexist context. It was grounded in my longing to see an end to forms of unnecessary suffering in black women's lives, in black people's lives. Given this background, I felt that my struggle to write such a book was itself a political gesture, an act of risk and daring. The research and writing was the site of much education for critical consciousness. Coming to understand the way in which sexism had shaped the experience and social status of black women was overwhelming and the world began to be a different place for me.

In its initial stages, the book was modeled after sociological texts and much of the writing was stiff, artificial, and wordy. This first draft of the book exposed many weaknesses in my consciousness as a writing subject. The major problem was that I was trying to speak to all possible audiences, to appease and placate. The writing of the book was complicated by the fact that I was a student and working a full-time job. After writing initial drafts, I went to work as a telephone operator in an office that was predominately black and female. Negative dimensions of black female experience, especially those experiences informed by sexism in our lives, were an ongoing topic of conversation. There, my conviction that black women and other people needed to understand the extent to which sexism was an oppressive force in black women's lives along with racism was deepened. This was an important year for work on the book because the black women I worked with daily felt that it was important that someone attempt to tell people about negative aspects of our social reality. They provided support and affirmation of the project, the kind of support I had not found in a university setting. They were not concerned about my credentials, about my writing skills, about degrees. They, like me, wanted someone to say the kinds of things about our lives that would bring change or further understanding.

After a year of working at the phone company, I began graduate school in English, an environment hostile to any graduate student who did not focus solely on literature. There I struggled to do my work as well as rewriting and rethinking the manuscript. When I talked to people about the work, they were not supportive. Many white people and even some black men wanted to know why it was important to talk about black women and my explanations were rarely persuasive enough. Even though most of them had never thought about the subject, they were confident they knew more than me. I was eager to have feedback about the ideas in the book and continued to discuss them despite so much negative feedback. It did not occur to me to look for a more "feminist" environment to work in. I did not think there was anything inappropriate about trying to integrate feminism and my work on black women and sexism into the environment in which I was living.

Now I think it was very important that I was not writing in a clearly defined, separate feminist environment because the majority of women, and certainly the majority of black women, do not live in such environments and must acquire the skill and strategies necessary to survive in a healthy and progressive manner wherever we are. In many ways, feminism as a political movement has been undermined by our inability to integrate feminist thinking and action in all social spaces. Having recently completed a new book in the context of an academic environment where I work as a lecturer in Women's Studies and where publications are seen as important (but not in terms of how they promote political change), I can see more clearly that how I wrote *Ain't I A Woman* was informed by my circumstances (coming home to try to write and think after an eight-hour day). This experience enabled me to know what it is like to be a social critic, or as Toni Cade Bambara put it, a "cultural worker" in the everyday world. The black women I was working with at the phone company wanted me to write a book that would make our lives better, one that would make other people understand the hardships of being black and female. It was different to be writing in a context where my ideas were not seen as separate from real people and real lives.

I think all of us, as black women, working non-management jobs at the phone company, felt ourselves to be constantly at the mercy of dominating structures. We were deeply aware of economic exploitation. It was in part the pain of that experience that sent me back to graduate school. Yet the book would probably never have been written were it not for that experience. I felt then that my heart was in the writing of *Ain't I A Woman,* that it was a book of the heart, expressing the deep and passionate longing for change in the social status of black women, for an end to sexist domination and exploitation. With the black women on the job I felt this longing to be understood—shared. I say this because I feel that the recent interest in black women's writing can obscure the reality that it has always been difficult for black women, especially black women who are working-class, to produce writing in this culture, especially writing of a radical political nature.

During the time that I was writing *Ain't I A Woman,* the years of rewriting and rethinking, I felt terribly discouraged about my individual lot as a black woman in the United States and most discouraged about our collective lot. While writing, I often felt an intense despair that was so overwhelming I really questioned how we could bear being alive in this society, how we could stay alive. I was profoundly discouraged by the many forces colluding to support the myth of the strong super-black woman, and it seemed that it would be impossible to compel recognition of black woman's exploitation and oppression. It is not that black women have not been and are not strong; it is simply that this is only a part of our story, a dimension, just as the suffering is another dimension—one that has been most unnoticed and unattended to. I have been in feminist groups where white women and black women would spend enormous energy talking about black women's strength and refuse to recognize its limitations. Recently, I invited a white feminist scholar who had published a book on black women to come and speak in my course on "Women and Race." Students noticed that a consistent image throughout her work was that of the "strong" black woman, and they were afraid to ask her the question that had most come to mind for them: If black women were so strong, why was it that her white female voice was the one articulating our history and not the voice of those strong black women who helped give material for the work, who gave interviews and told their stories?

When I finished *Ain't I A Woman,* with all the re-writing and rethinking, more than six years had passed. I sent it off to a number of publishers who rejected the work. Discouraged, I put the manuscript away. Then "race" became an important topic in feminist circles. It was important because white women had decided that they were ready to hear about race. When black women had been talking about race in our own way they did not deem it relevant. Significantly, this shift in feminist concerns created a context where I could find a publisher for *Ain't I A Woman.* One evening I gave a talk at the women's bookstore in San Francisco discussing my work. Our discussion was extremely heated as I addressed my anger that white supremacy within feminist movement meant that white women and not black women or other women of color could determine for us when race could be a subject for feminist discussion. At this talk, three white women told me they had seen an ad in a Bay area feminist newspaper from a publisher looking for work on race and feminism. I sent the book to South End and wanted them to publish it because they were a collective.

By its final re-writing, the book had become a serious polemic about black women and feminism. When the white woman editor at South End who was working with the manuscript first talked with me about the book, she told me that members of the collective felt it was a very angry book and were concerned that it did not have a positive bent. I responded by saying that though I had written in the direct blunt manner that is the customary mode of discourse in my black southern family, I was not angry. Our different perceptions of the implication of my speech, of my tone were important signifiers of the way in which race and class shape our ways of speaking and reading. Many outspoken black people have had an experience in which the passions, intensity, and conviction in our speech is interpreted by white listeners as anger. I think this is especially the case in a culture wherein people do not speak directly. And when one speaks directly and is also critical, it is likely to be seen as being an expression of hostility. This has to do with the attitude toward criticism that prevails in our society. Unfortunately most people feel that criticism is negative and is aimed at diminishing whatever is being critiqued. I was certainly adamant in *Ain't I A Woman* that black women had much to gain through participation in a feminist movement, even though I was equally adamant in my criticism of dominant tendencies in the movement that I felt undermined its importance. I did not see my book as representing "the" feminist work or "the" black female statement on feminism. It was and remains a polemical piece.

When the editor suggested that I make changes, that I be more positive, I refused. Already I had given more of my life to writing this book than should have ever been needed; I could not write more. I did not want to write about feminist movement in terms that would change my perspective, even though the Press felt the book was "too negative." Only on one issue did I agree to make changes and that concerned my critical comments about attempts by feminist activists to make lesbianism and feminism synonymous. Even though I argued with the Press that critical comments about the relationship of lesbianism to feminist politics does not necessarily imply hatred, or support of homophobia, I did agree that in a homophobic society to offer negative criticism exclusively could reinforce homophobia. Since I was not willing to work anew on the manuscript, I suggested that all such critical comments be removed and they were. In retrospect this does not seem to have been the only possible solution for it led many readers to assume that I wanted to deny the presence of lesbians in feminist movement, or that I was so homophobic I could not bring myself to say the word lesbian. Since the overall tone of the book was critical, it might have been better to state that critical comments about lesbianism and feminist movement were not intended to promote or encourage homophobia.

While feminist women (many of whom are white) often say that they want to hear from women who have not spoken, they do not always want to hear what we have to say. Often when we speak, our ideas are not only expressed differently but they are different and this difference is not always affirmed. To speak about feminism, those of us who are coming from different ethnic and racial backgrounds must first work to overcome the racism, sexism, and class exploitation that has socialized us to believe that our words are not important. It was hard for me to cling to the vision that writing about black women was important when so many people were suggesting it was not, when the many books I was reading suggested that we were not an important subject. For me, writing my first book was an act of self-recovery, a gesture of resistance. More than anything else, I wanted *Ain't I A Woman* to speak to the reality that sexism was and is an oppressive, exploitative force in black women's lives. That was the promise of the book for me—and that promise has been fulfilled.

22

writing autobiography

To me, telling the story of my growing up years was intimately connected with the longing to kill the self I was without really having to die. I wanted to kill that self in writing. Once that self was gone—out of my life forever—I could more easily become the me of me. It was clearly the Gloria Jean of my tormented and anguished childhood that I wanted to be rid of, the girl who was always wrong, always punished, always subjected to some humiliation or other, always crying, the girl who was to end up in a mental institution because she could not be anything but crazy, or so they told her. She was the girl who sat a hot iron on her arm pleading with them to leave her alone, the girl who wore her scar as a brand marking her madness. Even now I can hear the voices of my sisters saying "mama make Gloria stop crying." By writing the autobiography, it was not just this Gloria I would be rid of, but the past that had a hold on me, that kept me from the present. I wanted not to forget the past but to break its hold. This death in writing was to be liberatory.

Until I began to try and write an autobiography, I thought that it would be a simple task this telling of one's story. And yet I tried year after year, never writing more than a few pages. My inability to write out the story I interpreted as an indication that I was not ready to let go of the past, that I was not ready to be fully in the present. Psychologically, I considered the possibility that I had become attached to the wounds and sorrows of my childhood, that I held to them in a manner that blocked my efforts to be self-realized, whole, to be healed. A key message in Toni Cade Bambara's novel *The Salteaters*, which tells the story of Velma's suicide attempt, her breakdown, is expressed when the healer asks her "are you sure sweetheart, that you want to be well?"

There was very clearly something blocking my ability to tell my story. Perhaps it was remembered scoldings and punishments when mama heard me saying something to a friend or stranger that she did not think should be said. Secrecy and silence—these were central issues. Secrecy about family, about what went on in the domestic household was a bond between us—was part of what made us family. There was a dread one felt about breaking that bond. And yet I could not grow inside the atmosphere of secrecy that had pervaded our lives and the lives of other families about us. Strange that I had always challenged the secrecy, always let something slip that should not be known growing up, yet as a writer staring into the solitary space of paper, I was bound, trapped in the fear that a bond is lost or broken in the telling. I did not want to be the traitor, the teller of family secrets—and yet I wanted to be a writer. Surely, I told myself, I could write a purely imaginative work—a work that would not hint at personal private realities. And so I tried. But always there were the intruding traces, those elements of real life however disguised. Claiming the freedom to grow as an imaginative writer was connected for me with having the courage to open, to be able to tell the truth of one's life as I had experienced it in writing. To talk about one's life—that I could do. To write about it, to leave a trace—that was frightening.

The longer it took me to begin the process of writing autobiography, the further removed from those memories I was becoming. Each year, a memory seemed less and less clear. I wanted not to lose the vividness, the recall and felt an urgent need to begin the work and complete it. Yet I could not begin even though I had begun to confront some of the reasons I was blocked, as I am blocked just now in writing this piece because I am afraid to express in writing the experience that served as a catalyst for that block to move.

I had met a young black man. We were having an affair. It is important that he was black. He was in some mysterious way a link to this past that I had been struggling to grapple with, to name in writing. With him I remembered incidents, moments of the past that I had completely suppressed. It was as though there was something about the passion of contact that was hypnotic, that enabled me to drop barriers and thus enter fully, rather re-enter those past experiences. A key aspect seemed to be the way he smelled, the combined odors of cigarettes, occasionally alcohol, and his body smells. I thought often of the phrase "scent of memory," for it was those smells that carried me back. And there were specific occasions when it was very evident that the experience of being in his company was the catalyst for this remembering.

Two specific incidents come to mind. One day in the middle of the afternoon we met at his place. We were drinking cognac and dancing to music from the radio. He was smoking cigarettes (not only do I not smoke, but I usually make an effort to avoid smoke). As we held each other dancing those mingled odors of alcohol, sweat, and cigarettes led me to say, quite without thinking about it, "Uncle Pete." It was not that I had forgotten Uncle Pete. It was more that I had forgotten the childhood experience of meeting him. He drank often, smoked cigarettes, and always on the few occasions that we met him, he held us children in tight embraces. It was the memory of those embraces—of the way I hated and longed to resist them—that I recalled.

Another day we went to a favorite park to feed ducks and parked the car in front of tall bushes. As we were sitting there, we suddenly heard the sound of an oncoming train—a sound which startled me so that it evoked another long-suppressed memory: that of crossing the train tracks in my father's car. I recalled an incident where the car stopped on the tracks and my father left us sitting there while he raised the hood of the car and worked to repair it. This is an incident that I am not certain actually happened. As a child, I had been terrified of just such an incident occurring, perhaps so terrified that it played itself out in my mind as though it had happened. These are just two ways this encounter acted as a catalyst breaking down barriers enabling me to finally write this long-desired autobiography of my childhood.

Each day I sat at the typewriter and different memories were written about in short vignettes. They came in a rush, as though they were a sudden thunderstorm. They came in a surreal, dreamlike style which made me cease to think of them as strictly autobiographical because it seemed that myth, dream, and reality had merged. There were many incidents that I would talk about with my siblings to see if they recalled them. Often we remembered together a general outline of an incident but the details were different for us. This fact was a constant reminder of the limitations of autobiography, of the extent to which autobiography is a very personal story telling—a unique recounting of events not so much as they have happened but as we remember and invent them. One memory that I would have sworn was "the truth and nothing but the truth" concerned a wagon that my brother and I shared as a child. I remembered that we played with this toy only at my grandfather's house, that we shared it, that I would ride it and my brother would push me. Yet one facet of the memory was puzzling, I remembered always returning home with bruises or scratches from this toy. When I called my mother, she said there had never been any wagon, that we had shared a red wheelbarrow, that it had always been at my grandfather's house because there were sidewalks on that part of town. We lived in the hills where there were no sidewalks. Again I was compelled to face the fiction that is a part of all retelling, remembering. I began to think of the work I was doing as both fiction and autobiography. It seemed to fall in the category of writing that Audre Lorde, in her autobiographically-based work *Zami,* calls bio-mythography. As I wrote, I felt that I was not as concerned with accuracy of detail as I was with evoking in writing the state of mind, the spirit of a particular moment.

The longing to tell one's story and the process of telling is symbolically a gesture of longing to recover the past in such a way that one experiences both a sense of reunion and a sense of release. It was the longing for release that compelled the writing but concurrently it was the joy of reunion that enabled me to see that the act of writing one's autobiography is a way to find again that aspect of self and experience that may no longer be an actual part of one's life but is a living memory shaping and informing the present. Autobiographical writing was a way for me to evoke the particular experience of growing up southern and black in segregated communities. It was a way to recapture the richness of southern black culture. The need to remember and hold to the legacy of that experience and what it taught me has been all the more important since I have since lived in predominately white communities and taught at predominately white colleges. Black southern folk experience was the foundation of the life around me when I was a child; that experience no longer exists in many places where it was once all of life that we knew. Capitalism, upward mobility, assimilation of other values have all led to rapid disintegration of black folk experience or in some cases the gradual wearing away of that experience.

Within the world of my childhood, we held onto the legacy of a distinct black culture by listening to the elders tell their stories. Autobiography was experienced most actively in the art of telling one's story. I can recall sitting at Baba's (my grandmother on my mother's side) at 1200 Broad Street—listening to people come and recount their life experience. In those days, whenever I brought a playmate to my grandmother's house, Baba would want a brief outline of their autobiography before we would begin playing. She wanted not only to know who their people were but what their values were. It was sometimes an awesome and terrifying experience to stand answering these questions or witness another playmate being subjected to the process and yet this was the way we would come to know our own and one another's family history. It is the absence of such a tradition in my adult life that makes the written narrative of my girlhood all the more important. As the years pass and these glorious memories grow much more vague, there will remain the clarity contained within the written words.

Conceptually, the autobiography was framed in the manner of a hope chest. I remembered my mother's hope chest, with its wonderful odor of cedar and thought about her taking the most precious items and placing them there for safekeeping. Certain memories were for me a similar treasure. I wanted to place them somewhere for safekeeping. An autobiographical narrative seemed an appropriate place. Each particular incident, encounter, experience had its own story, sometimes told from the first person, sometimes told from the third person. Often I felt as though I was in a trance at my typewriter, that the shape of a particular memory was decided not by my conscious mind but by all that is dark and deep within me, unconscious but present. It was the act of making it present, bringing it into the open, so to speak, that was liberating.

From the perspective of trying to understand my psyche, it was also interesting to read the narrative in its entirety after I had completed the work. It had not occurred to me that bringing one's past, one's memories together in a complete narrative would allow one to view them from a different perspective, not as singular isolated events but as part of a continuum. Reading the completed manuscript, I felt as though I had an overview not so much of my childhood but of those experiences that were deeply imprinted in my consciousness. Significantly, that which was absent, left out, not included also was important. I was shocked to find at the end of my narrative that there were few incidents I recalled that involved my five sisters. Most of the incidents with siblings were with me and my brother. There was a sense of alienation from my sisters present in childhood, a sense of estrangement. This was reflected in the narrative. Another aspect of the completed manuscript that is interesting to me is the way in which the incidents describing adult men suggest that I feared them intensely, with the exception of my grandfather and a few old men. Writing the autobiographical narrative enabled me to look at my past from a different perspective and to use this knowledge as a means of self-growth and change in a practical way.

In the end I did not feel as though I had killed the Gloria of my childhood. Instead I had rescued her. She was no longer the enemy within, the little girl who had to be annihilated for the woman to come into being. In writing about her, I reclaimed that part of myself I had long ago rejected, left uncared for, just as she had often felt alone and uncared for as a child. Remembering was part of a cycle of reunion, a joining of fragments, "the bits and pieces of my heart" that the narrative made whole again.

23

to gloria, who is she: on using a pseudonym

It is the end of my first year of full-time teaching. At a farewell dinner to celebrate, to say goodbye for a few months, I propose a toast "to gloria, who is she." Amid the laughter of friends I can raise the question of identity, of naming. Since I write using a pseudonym, I am often confronted by readers seeking an explanation. At this very farewell party naming comes into play because to one person present I am known by the pseudonym bell hooks. It was initially only a name for writing—then I began to use it when I gave lectures to avoid confusion.

bell hooks is a name that comes from family. It is the name of my great-grandmother on my mother's side. In the beginning, I took this name because I was publishing a small book of poems in a community where someone else had the same given name. It was then mostly a practical choice—one I could easily make because I had not been attached to the name "Gloria." It had always seemed a name that was not me, evoking much that I am not. As I grew older, I began to associate this name with frivolity and dizziness (as in the stereotype of the dumb blonde, often named Gloria). Even though I am sometimes dizzy and quite frivolous, I was afraid then that this name would take me over, become my identity before I could make it what I wanted it to be. I welcomed the chance to choose and use another name.

I chose the name bell hooks because it was a family name, because it had a strong sound. Throughout childhood, this name was used to speak to the memory of a strong woman, a woman who spoke her mind. Then in the segregated world of our black community—a strong woman was someone able to make her own way in this world, a woman who possessed traits often associated only with men—she would kill for family and honor—she would do whatever was necessary to survive—she would be true to her word. Claiming this name was a way to link my voice to an ancestral legacy of woman speaking—of woman power. When I first used this name with poetry, no one ever questioned this use of a pseudonym, perhaps because the realm of imaginative writing is deemed more private than social.

When I began writing *Ain't I A Woman: Black Women and Feminism,* the pseudonym began to play a very different role in my life as a writer. Gloria, as I thought of her, as I became her, was not someone particularly concerned with politics. I was more concerned then with the contemplative life, with the inner struggle for self-realization, for spiritual enlightenment. When I began to think about political issues, about feminist politics, I had difficulty reconciling this new passion with the pattern of my life. I saw myself then as a poet who, though addressing political issues in my writing, was not seeking a public voice. When I wrote the first draft of *Ain't I A Woman,* I was nineteen years old, and it was an extremely long manuscript, more than 500 pages. Reading it I could hear in the writing no voice I could claim to be my own. Instead the voices in the text seemed to vary according to which group was being talked about: white women, black men, black women, white men. There were so many voices because I was afraid to have my voice stand alone. I was afraid of saying the wrong thing. Fear of saying or doing that which will be considered "wrong" often inhibits people who are members of exploited and/or oppressed groups. This inhibiting factor acts to suppress and stifle creativity both in terms of critical thinking and artistic expression. Much of what we say is tempered and contained by fear of saying that which might be considered "wrong," and what constitutes it being wrong is the likelihood of punishment. In childhood, I was often punished for saying the wrong thing, for thinking in ways that the grown-ups around me did not consider appropriate. This early socialization had a tremendous impact on my capacity for self-expression.

Many individuals from oppressed groups learn to suppress ideas, especially those deemed oppositional, as a survival strategy. From slavery on, black people in the United States have learned to be guarded in our speech. Saying the wrong thing could lead to severe punishment or death. This pattern of guarded expression continued long after slavery ended. Since racial oppression remained a social norm, black people still found it necessary to check freedom of expression, to engage in self-censorship. Many older black people were raised in racially segregated environments

wherein saying the wrong thing, especially to a white person, could lead
to punishment. Often our elders would say that they were punishing us to
teach us our place, to keep us in line, so that we would not be punished
by white people, so that we would not be destroyed. Such attitudes have
had a profound impact on the way black children are raised, on our capacity
for creative expression.

When I contemplate this, an image comes to mind of a black woman
I got to know because we both were frequent shoppers at a Salvation Army
thrift store—as in we would be there every day. She would often bring a
very young grandchild to the store, a girl of three or four. This child would
be told to sit very still until it was time to return home, even if her
grandmother shopped for hours. She was not allowed to talk, laugh, or
play and certainly not to move around. She only spoke when given permission. I noticed how often white and black people alike made favorable
comments about the obedience, the "good" behavior of this little girl. I
wondered what would happen to her in school, if she would be unable to
speak, afraid to speak. Would she ever recover the wildly creative spaces
inside herself after years of learning silence, obedience? It is not an easy
legacy to undo.

After years of being told that I said the wrong thing, of being
punished, I had to struggle to find my own voice, to feel that I could speak
without being punished. Writing *Ain't I A Woman,* I was compelled to confront this fear of expression. This effort seemed to be impossible. How
could Gloria find her voice, speak firmly and directly when I was so accustomed to finding veiled ways of expression, abstract, unclear ways? For
me, the pseudonym had a very therapeutic function. Through the use of
the name bell hooks I was able to claim an identity that affirmed for me
my right to speech. Gloria as I had constructed her was meant to lead a
monastic, spiritual life or a solitary reclusive writer's life; she was not to be
a writer of feminist books. Again it is important to remember that I was
nineteen when I began this writing. Bell hooks could write feminist books
and have a voice. And it seems to me quite fitting that this was a good old-
fashioned 19th century name. Black female intellectual traditions were
strong during that century. Women like Anna Cooper, Frances Ellen Harper, and Mary Church Terrell were giving expression to the radical vision
of black women concerned with politics, with struggles for liberation. It
was fitting and appropriate for me to draw strength and courage from an
unknown 19th century black woman whose legacy of strong and serious
speech was carried on in oral history, was remembered. Bell hooks as I
came to know her through this sharing of family history, as I dreamed and
invented her, became a symbol of what I could become, all that my parents
had hoped little Gloria would never be. Gloria was to have been a sweet
southern girl, quiet, obedient, pleasing. She was not to have that wild streak
that characterized women on my mother's side. Indeed it seemed my

mother Rosa Bell was proud that she had learned to control her wild and creative impulses, that she would obey and conform.

Choosing this name as a pseudonym was a rebellious gesture. It was part of a strategy of empowerment, enabling me to surrender Gloria, give her back to those who had created her, so that I could make and find my own voice, my identity. Though eager to surrender the obedient aspect of who Gloria was meant to be, I did not want to surrender my belief in the primacy of spirituality as a life force. These beliefs were further inducement to use a pseudonym. Much of the religious thought that moved me emphasized letting go of the ego, the ever present I, of non-attachment. Using the pseudonym was a constant reminder that my ideas were expressions of me but they were not the whole picture. I did not want to become over-identified with these ideas, so attached to them that I would be unable or unwilling to change perspectives, to let them go if necessary, to admit errors in my thinking. This was particularly important as many assumptions I had about black women's experiences were challenged by new material I found. To be made continually aware that I was not creating an identity for myself in this work—only sharing ideas—was crucial to my intellectual growth. In academic settings, I have witnessed the extreme attachment scholars often have to their ideals, often acting as though they are possessions, property, to be owned, controlled, maintained at all costs. Among feminist thinkers, I have witnessed the reluctance to change perceptions about the nature of white female experience, of the women's rights movement in the United States. Often it seemed over-identification with ideas, seeing them as not merely expressions of one's self but as absolute representations of the self, blocked creative, critical thinking and intellectual growth. In using the pseudonym, I consciously sought to make a separation between ideas and identity so that I could be open to challenge and change.

Though by no means a solution to this problem, a pseudonym certainly creates a distance between the published work and the author. On the level of experimentation, I was curious about the ways using a pseudonym would affect the way I saw myself—the way I saw the work. Initially, I was not certain that it would enable me to feel a distance between not only myself and the published work but responses to that work. It occurred to me that this artificially created distance might have little impact. This proved not to be the case. When the published book first arrived by mail, I held it in my hand, looking at the name bell hooks and felt a distance I knew would not be there if my given name had been on the cover. Then looking at the cover layout, I considered the link between bell hooks and the title; bell hooks was written in small letter without capitals, *Ain't I A Woman* was all capitals. For me issues of identity were raised by the absence of quotation marks around the question "ain't i a woman," no comment on the inner pages that would claim these words as property of Sojourner Truth, whose given name Isabelle Bumfree was discarded, as she asserted that when she left slavery she wanted to leave all signs of bondage behind. With the name Sojourner Truth, she evoked her new revolutionary political calling as well as her spiritual work—a liberatory name. Within contemporary feminist movement, the name Sojourner Truth and the phrase "ain't i a woman" had been quite appropriated, used, and exploited in much the same way that the labor of black women has been used and exploited in a white-supremacist, capitalist patriarchy. Significantly, I did not think that I would be masking Sojourner Truth's identity or laying claim to her words as though they were my own, but rather I sought to lay claim to the experience they evoked, to shift the attention away from personal identity, speaker, back to the words themselves and the meaning they evoked. It was my sense that this phrase was still a question contemporary black women have been compelled to raise as we confront a racist and sexist society that would deny our womanness.

Longing to shift attention away from personality, from self, to ideas, informed my use of a pseudonym. Cults of personality had, from my perspective, severely limited feminist movement, as often we seemed to be more engaged by who was speaking/writing than by what they were saying. Living as we do in a culture that promotes narcissism, that encourages it because it deflects attention away from our capacity to form political commitments that address issues rather than identity, I wanted to construct a work that would place distance between personality, identity of speaker, and that spoken about. It was my hope that the text would be more compelling, read not through preconceived perceptions and ideas about the writer. Since bell hooks was an unknown writer and thinker, it was impossible for readers to refer to a personality. The point of the pseudonym was not to mask, to hide my identity but rather to shift the focus, to make it less relevant. The book was copyrighted in my given name, and that name appeared on the copyright page. When the work was first published, a few critical readers suggested that I used a pseudonym to avoid assuming responsibility for this horrible, outrageous work. Unlike the realm of imaginative writing, the use of a pseudonym to do work that was scholarly, to do social criticism, was deemed inappropriate and unacceptable, a suspicious action. One press agreed to publish the book if I would not use the pseudonym. Such responses enabled a few critics to place even more value on personal identity as a means of reinforcing their critiques. Ironically, in many ways the use of the pseudonym failed as a strategy shifting attention away from personality. As the book became more widely read, as readers wanted to know more about the author, as I began to publicly discuss the work, I was constantly asked to explain my use of a pseudonym. It was particularly discouraging when that would be the primary subject audiences would want to discuss after a lecture. And I am writing this in part as a response to this questioning.

Within a capitalist consumer society, the cult of personality has the power to subsume ideas, to make the person, the personality into the product and not the work itself. Advertising and marketing strategies reinforce the emphasis on the person as product. When this is coupled with the longing writers have for recognition, for acknowledgement of our presence as well as our work, we are vulnerable to exploitation. It is this area of ego that makes possible a narcissistic focus on self that can, as my grandmother would say, lead to soul loss. Recently, I heard black woman writer Ann Petry, now in her later seventies, speak about how cults of personality, especially as they affect a writer's life, encourage a fragmentation of self that threatens one's capacity to be whole. Speaking of her own enormous success in the 1940s, she addressed ways the public's focus on her personal life began to obscure her identity as thinker and writer. It was especially moving to hear her speak about ways so much focus on her personal identity at the time made her feel as though she was leaving bits and pieces of herself here and there. Using the pseudonym has been for me a way to avoid making myself into "product." It is part of an ongoing effort to maintain my inner well-being while engaging in a process of public sharing both through my work and through public discussion.

Using the pseudonym has not really changed the reader's focus on writer identity, on the personality of an author, as much as I had hoped it might. Yet it did lead to greater awareness about the relationship between author, identity, and a text. Even without information about bell hooks, readers often shared with me the identity they construct based on the name and the way the work is written. It has been interesting for me to arrive at places where bell hooks is scheduled to talk and find people waiting for her to appear—certain that there will be something about the way she presents herself, something that her name, her work has suggested that will allow them to know her: how she will look, how she will carry herself. I know this because many people have generously shared their impressions. Often women tell me that they imagine bell hooks will be a large woman with a powerful voice. And I wonder whether such perceptions are informed by stereotypical images of black womanhood where the assertive black female, who speaks her mind, is portrayed as physically grotesque. On other occasions, I witness the disappointment of readers who have invented a presence for bell hooks that I do not embody, readers who feel let down or even betrayed by the real me. The interface between me as real person and invisible author forces me to examine our obsessions with personality, with the representations of self. Recently I entered a kitchen filled with black women waiting to welcome bell hooks; the first expression was one of surprise. I was not as imagined. We had a fun discussion of how folks had imagined I might be and talked about ways we place so much emphasis, too much, on how people appear.

Another aspect of using the pseudonym is that I often hear perspectives on my work from folks who do not initially know that they are speaking to the author. This is at times very disconcerting and often quite funny. Like the time a black male reader sat at a friend's house intensely arguing with me about feminism, telling me that I should read bell hooks. Or when I moved recently and my next door neighbor, helping me carry junk into the flat, talked about feminist works, giving a great review of *Ain't I A Woman* which she encouraged me to read. It was a pleasure to share with her my thoughts about this work. I describe these little incidents of which there are many more, because they have been a part of the experience, the constructive play, that using a pseudonym engages one in and with. Inevitably these interactions raise serious questions about naming and identity.

Naming is a serious process. It has been of crucial concern for many individuals within oppressed groups who struggle for self-recovery, for self-determination. It has been important for black people in the United States. Think of the many African-American slaves who renamed themselves after emancipation or the use of nicknames in traditional folk communities, where such names act to tell something specific about the bearer. Within many folk traditions globally, among the Inuit, the Australian Aborigines, naming is a source of empowerment, an important gesture in the process of creation. A primacy is given to naming as a gesture that deeply shapes and influences the social construction of a self. As in southern African-American folk traditions, a name is perceived as a force that has the power to determine whether or not an individual will be fully self-realized, whether she or he will be able to fulfill their destiny, find their place in the world.

To me naming is about empowerment. It is also a source of tremendous pleasure. I name everything—typewriters, cars, most things I use—that gives something to me. It is a way to acknowledge the life force in every object. Often the names I give to things and people are related to my past. They are a way to preserve and honor aspects of that past. Speaking of ancestor acknowledgement within African traditions has been a way to talk about how we learn from folks we may never have known but who live again in us. In Western traditions, this same process is talked about as the collective unconscious, the means by which we inherit the wisdom and ways of our ancestors. Talking with an elderly black man about names, he reminded me that in our southern black folk tradition we have the belief that a person never dies as long as their name is remembered, called. When the name bell hooks is called, the spirit of my great-grandmother rises.

24

interview

It would not be an exaggeration to say that Gloria Watkins is the focus of a great deal of controversy, criticism, praise and curiosity by nearly all sectors of the Yale community. Both of her classes this year have received double or triple the enrollment expected of them, and a talk given by her at the Law School in February drew so many people it had to be moved to a bigger room, which was still unable to accommodate the crowd. As a student in her Afro-American Literature class last term, I quickly learned that Gloria is not your typical Yale professor. As she herself explains in this interview, she likes to challenge—both others and herself. It is this constant challenging of accepted societal norms that makes Gloria Watkins an inspiring lecturer, a thought-provoking author of radical feminist theory, and a favorite topic of dinner-time conversation.

The following is an interview I had with Gloria on March 24th, in which she talked about her books, her lecture at the Law School (which was titled "We long to be loved and we long to be free; we long to be free and we long to be loved."), and her views on "the politics of domination."

Yvonne Zylan

* * *

YZ: You mentioned before that you received a lot of criticism about the absence of a discussion of lesbianism after *Ain't I A Woman?*...

167

GW: Well, I think it's legitimate critique to raise the question of why there isn't a discussion of lesbianism and it's real complicated. Barbara [Smith] and other people have accused me of homophobia. I remember when I first met Adrienne Rich, she said, "I don't like what you did to lesbians in *Ain't I A Woman?*, and I said, "What did I do?" There was the whole sense that I was being homophobic through silencing. I think of homophobia as people who are both afraid of and prejudiced against people who are gay. Certainly silence *can* be an expression of that. In the case of *Ain't I A Woman?*, as you know from reading it, it is a polemical book—I am critical of practically everyone, and needless to say, when lesbians appeared in the book (which they did in the original manuscript) it was in a critical context, and my editor at that time, a lesbian white woman, felt that I should say more positive things about lesbian women. Basically, I was critiquing the whole equation of feminism and lesbianism and also raising the question of whether or not, to some extent, lesbian women have more at stake in the feminist movement in the sense of building culture, and building different places of meeting, etc. Our struggle was that she was saying "I think if you're going to say these critical things you should say something positive." At that point, I was sick of writing. I mean, this was years of writing, I said, "uh uh, I don't want to write anything else." But I said "I realize this is a homophobic culture" and to say critical things about gay people without saying positive things does, in fact, lead you to run the risk of perpetuating homophobia. So I took out every single comment in which the word gay or lesbian was used, and so you have Cheryl Clarke saying about me in *Home Girls* that, you know, bell hooks is so homophobic she can't bring herself to use the word lesbian. I didn't put "lesbian" before their names, does that mean that I'm silencing them? I said, "You know, I didn't put *anyone's* sexual preference before their names...." I mean to me these issues are all so complex. I think that there were real ideological differences that kind of got obscured under this more general critique of homophobia.

YZ: Do you think that critique influenced you when you were writing *Feminist Theory: from margin to center* because obviously there's a lot more mention of heterosexism and homophobia and how they affect—
GW: I think that one of the things that I had to come to grips with was that everything is a process. I think we have to remember that *Ain't I A Woman?*, I started writing it at 19.... I did a lot of the writing of it in Palo Alto and Wisconsin and certainly by the time I came to *Feminist Theory: from margin to center*, living in the Bay Area, and having classes of students that were predominantly lesbian, and living part-time with a lesbian couple in San Francisco, I mean my whole perspective had altered in many ways and had, as well, expanded through the whole process of learning and interaction, teaching at San Francisco State. I think a lot of those experiences

formed *Feminist Theory: from margin to center*. I don't want to make light of the fact that I was really hurt, deeply hurt, as somebody who had always felt, very much, herself to be anti-homophobic and struggling always in day-to-day life to counter homophobia. I was really crushed. I'll never forget that I happened to be particularly down on the day that I went to the bookstore and I saw *Home Girls* and I turned right to that passage where Cheryl Clarke said that I was so homophobic, and I just started screaming, and crying. I felt so hurt that, on the basis of their analysis of this book, people would begin to just make these incredible statements about me as a person.... I think we all need to be really careful when we sling out labels like this on the basis of something people write, especially something like *Ain't I A Woman?*, where the sin has to do with what I didn't say, as opposed to what I did say. Like, for example, not a single person of the people who made these critiques ever called me and said, "Why didn't you have comments about lesbianism in your book?"

Z: Let's talk a little about your talk at the Law School last month. There was quite a bit of open hostility, at the end during the question-and-answer period, and there seems to be a certain amount of hostility toward the way you approach teaching and the material that you're discussing. You talked in ...*margin to center* about, time after time, where there's hostility and anger and tears that can be an effective way of changing or helping somebody or yourself to come to a new perspective. Is there a conscious attempt on your part to spark that kind of confrontation?

W: Not at all. There *is* always a conscious attempt on my part to challenge. I mean there is not a day of my life that I am not critiquing myself and looking at myself to see if my politics are borne out in the way that I live and the way that I talk and present myself. I think that one of the best readings of *Ain't I A Woman?* for me came from a white woman student at Santa Cruz, a graduate student, Katie King, who said that, what she felt was that what I was always asking of people was that they shift their paradigms, and that whenever you ask people to shift their paradigms, they respond with hostility. I did not ever feel that I was hostile [at the Law School talk]. I feel that I very much asserted power, and I don't feel that I asserted it with the intent to dominate, but I did assert it. It seems to me that we, as women, have a lot of difficulty with the whole issue of assertion of power. I often feel that a lot of the hostility that people feel towards me is that we simply do live in a world where women don't often assert power, and that people get pissed off when women do. I feel that women particularly are not allowed to be non-nurturing in our styles. I mean people will praise male professors who have eccentric styles, or what have you, but those same characteristics in a woman become subject to real scrutiny and critique. I feel like in the talk I had been very open, very compassionate and very vulnerable. I was none of those things in the question-and-answer period. I was fatigued, and as I became fatigued, I became less willing to take on the whole burden of the discussion. One of the things I said was that in most cases I tried to throw people's questions back to them, but see, there again, we work within a paradigm where, usually, speakers are very nurturing during question-and-answer periods, very receptive, or they put on an air of receptivity, and I didn't put on an air of receptivity at all. I was surprised at myself, in that I've never felt such a split before, but I think that the *talk* was very difficult for me. I think that people did not really cut me a great deal of slack in terms of the difficulty of talking about male domination at a place where people are certainly not talking about male domination every day, and the difficulty of giving a paper at a place where you talk about your personal life as well—how many people try to integrate personal experience with their theoretical and analytical work here? Not many. All of those things made that talk very, very stressful. It's interesting to me that I said several times before the talk, even, that I was tired, but that did not in any way cause people to shift their expectations. I was impressed by the fact that most of the feedback I got was about the question-and-answer period and not the talk itself.

YZ: Do you find that that's often the case, that the way you present something, deflects attention away from what you're saying?

GW: Yes, and I think we have to be really suspicious of that—people don't want to deal with male domination—how convenient to turn a discussion of male domination into a critique of me. Just recently I gave a talk at a black women's film festival, and it was interesting, because the topic was supposed to be on black women and finding a black female voice. The audience and the panel members never focused on black women. But that seems logical in a culture where black women are at the very bottom of the social and economic totem pole. And so I had to say to people that they would have to take a minute and examine how we're interacting here because every time the topic of black women comes up, we switch it to something else. I wanted us to examine what was our own difficulty in actually talking about black women, in taking the black woman's experience seriously. It seems to me that this happens a lot with feminist concerns. People deflect away from them in all kinds of ways.

YZ: You talked in *Ain't I A Woman* and in *...from margin to center* about the question that people are always asking you: Which is more important to a black woman, a question of racism or a question of sexism? And you seem to be making the point that they are interlocked and are of equal importance, and yet, in some of your arguments, there's a sense of primacy to questions of racism, that it is more endemic to our society, the structures which dominate and oppress people.

GW: Well, one of the things that I definitely tried to say is that we've seen a great many more structural changes in the position of women, and especially white women, and privileged women in our culture than we could say about race. Certainly feminist struggle is not nearly as old as the struggle against racism in this culture. I think to say that they are of equal importance does not belie the fact that there are also occasions in which one may be more important. I mean, as I grow older, I find that issues of sexism and gender domination obsess my psyche a lot more and that's because a lot of the kinds of things that I've struggled with around race, have become, as I have established myself, less problematic than interpersonal issues of domination, etc. And I think we ought to be willing to allow for the possibility that at different moments in one's life, one issue has primacy over another.

YZ: In ...*margin* you talk about the things that are divisive in terms of "Sisterhood" and the false sense of bonding upon shared oppression, but isn't that shared oppression, or that perception of shared oppression what brings women together around feminism in the first place? Isn't it necessary?

GW: It doesn't seem to be, Yvonne, in terms of black and white women, because our senses of oppression are so different. Or let's say, white women and women of color. I think that, again, it's a kind of complex thing. I think back to some of the sessions I've had in the past week, where groups of us as black women sat around and talked about different things that were going on in our lives. There was a sense of bonding because of the similarity of those experiences, but I think that if there had been a white woman in the room, the sense of that sharedness would have changed, because a lot of what we were talking about was influenced by both race and sex oppression. One can, of course, find a basis of bonding in shared experience and shared experience of oppression, but that is not the kind of bonding that will really transcend race, class, and ethnic lines. I think that is one form of bonding that can still exist for us, but I think we have to insist on a bonding that is about political commitment to feminism. And, I tell you, having come out of a strong feminist context, both in living experience and work experience, in California, to here—when I get into non-feminist environments, the difference is so incredible to me. I mean, I was on a panel recently with two women who were not committed to feminism—this made such a difference in how we dealt with each other as women and how the discussion went. To me, it's really wonderful and beautiful to bond with women in shared commitment to feminism—and with men.

YZ: It seems that one thing that comes up repeatedly in your arguments is the idea that bourgeois white women, who were involved in organizing contemporary feminism, taking control, etc., became involved in feminism as a means to get access to the privileges that only men could enjoy in the capitalist system. You talk about women who are in power not doing anything different with that power, they're doing what men do....Do you think that this is some fundamental flaw in contemporary feminism, that it was founded as a vehicle for getting more out of the capitalist system for women?

GW: I think that it's important that people read works like Zillah Eisenstein's *The Radical Future of Liberal Feminism* that try to document for us the fact that it's a liberal movement and that is places a great deal of emphasis on reform. I mean, the civil rights movement, as well, placed a great deal of emphasis on reform. And I think it has been a tradition that, other than Communist or other anti-capitalist movements, most reform movements under capitalism have had as a basic intent that one will struggle for some of the privileges that those in power have. So, in this way, I don't see contemporary feminist movement as unique, but at the same time, I think it was, tremendously, a basis of a movement that would automatically exclude a great many people. I mean, look at some of the symbolic gestures we see naming the beginning of the movement: the bra-burning, protesting the Miss America Pageant.... What if our symbolic gestures were women at a factory protesting working conditions? This would have a far more radical impact on our consciousness than the image of people burning a bra or some of the other symbolic gestures that came to be seen by popular media as indications of the direction of feminist movement. And though people would say, "Well, that isn't what it was ever about," that isn't even important, if those become the symbols that the mass audience of people know. In a sense, if that's how people perceive feminism, we still have to deal with that. Why didn't we want other symbols that would have been more striking to us, in terms of their political intent.

YZ: You did critique in ...*margin to center* Zillah Eisenstein's contention that there is radical potential in liberal feminism. Do you think that there isn't because of that kind of...

GW: Well, I don't think that there's radical potential in any movement where people imagine that we can hold onto class privilege under capitalism and have radical change. I think there's a lot of useful stuff in Zillah's book, but I simply don't see the bearing out of the ideas that she sets forth, because, theoretically, if she were right in her analysis, we would be witnessing this radical breakthrough and what we're witnessing is just the opposite, a regression. A moving away from feminist concerns, as opposed to an aggressive push to radicalism that she implied in that text.

YZ: In your chapter, "Rethinking the Nature of Work," you talked about the fact that there's no appeal in this idea of women going out and getting jobs to liberate themselves—for poor women, non-white women, lower-class women. Is this an indication that there is no value in women who do not hold paying jobs establishing some amount of economic independence? Or is there no liberatory potential in work, given the capitalist context?

GW: The primary thing I was trying to say is that, for people who work for very low wages, there is no economic self-sufficiency to be found in work.

The fact is, you make just enough to get by, so the sense that you are actually working toward something that will allow you to have a degree of freedom of movement or freedom of options, material options or otherwise, just isn't there for people. There's not the sense that work is really going to liberate you to have some time. Let's say you've been in a marriage, where you work part-time and you feel oppressed in that marriage, but your income joined with that of your spouse allows you some time; some time to go shopping, some time to go for a walk in the park, some time to read. What's going to motivate you to want to give that up—even though you may feel oppressed, or depressed, or repressed in that marriage—for a situation where you're going to have to work so many more hours per week and not have any kind of economic flexibility or time flexibility? There was a sort of lie in the fact that so much of the emphasis on work within the feminist movement really had to do with careers, which are by their very nature, so different from the kind of work most people do. If you come into the workforce with a Ph.D., or other skills that you can utilize, you're not talking about getting a very low-paying job for 40 hours a week. In my own life, coming from years of making a very low wage, because I've been working part-time for the last, what, 5 or 6 years, it's exciting to [now] make a wage that gives me flexibility, where I can send some money home, or take a trip, or do something. That kind of work is, I think, experienced by people as liberatory. But the kind of work you do where you do it and at the end of the month you still don't have any money, your life hasn't altered in any kind of significant way, you just simply don't experience that as liberatory. (pause…laughter) Make sure you put this laughter in. (more laughter)

YZ: You discuss the divisive effect of classism, racism, and sexism on female solidarity, and I don't want to beat this into the ground, but what about heterosexism? It seems to be conspicuously absent…
GW: Well, now, I've had a lot of arguments with people about this. I feel that a critique of heterosexism, to me, is included in the notion of sexism. I don't see heterosexism as being a separate category, because it seems to me that heterosexism is definitely the child of sexism. It is the child of gender oppression. I mean, when I think about sexism as a sort of general category of patriarchy, I do tend to think of there being all these subheadings, like homophobia. I mean, if you want to have this little world where men and women marry as part of your sexist vision, then it just seems to me that homophobia will necessarily be one of the modes of thought that you will encourage. I've had arguments with people who have felt very strongly that it simply isn't covered by that. I think that we haven't insisted on the reality that heterosexism is a central dimension of what sexism is.

YZ: But doesn't it, in its specific manifestations, in terms of its divisiveness between women, merit some *explicit* mention—

GW: Yes, I think that certainly the arguments I made would have been strengthened by talking about that...I like very much the terms "woman-identified" and "male-identified," and not in terms of them as indicative of sexual preference, but in terms of who you place at the center of your actions, your sense of self, or what have you. I remember [in one of my classes in California] in which students were lamenting that I did not have a lesbian identity and some of the students were saying that they felt really bad because they felt that a strong feminist like myself should be a lesbian. Betty, the black lesbian woman that I lived with said, "Gloria is a woman-identified woman whose affectional interests lie with a man." I think that the general sense of feeling care for *all* women, that whenever you see a woman in distress you feel some sense of unity is what I think of when I think of being woman-identified. Whenever I'm in non-feminist circles, speaking, I can really get a sense of what that is, in terms of women taking care of women, in terms of women *acknowledging* women. At this one conference I was at recently, I was struck by how the different women panel members never looked at one another. They would look directly at men, and talk to men and cater to the interests of men, etc. If we had all been woman-identified in that room [at the black women's film festival] we wouldn't been struggling around the issue of why we couldn't place black women at the center of the discourse. The sense that "the real feminist is a lesbian" came out of that whole feeling about what it means to be woman-identified. As you probably know, there are many lesbian woman who do not feel that sense of political solidarity with women.

YZ: And you discussed in your [Law School] talk about the lesbian who dresses like a man, and takes on those accoutrements of power. Is that the male-identified woman?

GW: Well, I used to, with good buddies, talk about these women, we used to call them "daddy's girls" because a lot of them were women who grew up identifying with their fathers and really, actually, hating their mothers. I mean, I know one of those women who used to say always that she just couldn't stand her mother's helplessness, and her role model of power was from her father. And these women can be found around—they may have sex with women, but a lot of their good buddies are males, and in fact they feel stronger identification with males than with women. And in a sense, they become honorary males who, like men, sleep with women, but who in a sense don't have a feeling of overall respect for women, and in fact may have a tremendous sense of contempt toward any woman who does not have the same style of strength and assertiveness, etc., etc. I remember the period of my life when I thought I wanted people to take me more seriously, as an undergraduate. I felt the real need to like, have short hair, and to wear a certain kind of clothing that did not suggest sensuality or sexuality. I mean, one of the things that I would say is that most male clothing does not evoke sexuality or sensuality, especially if we think about the colors of male clothing. Take, say, the business suit as a symbol, a clothing symbol of male power or even, say, the kind of clothing I was talking about in my talk, the uniforms of working-class men. My father was a janitor at the Post Office in our town for more than about 30 years and the clothing he wore was always drab. There's no suggestion of sexuality and sensuality in that clothing. In a sense, one of the things that we know is that it is the role of women to be sexual and sensual, and it is the role of men, that is, under patriarchy and within sexism, to conquer that sexuality. It's embedded as a signifier in the clothing that we wear. I know when I wanted to be taken seriously as a thinking, intellectual young woman, I felt the need to sort of destroy those signs of sensuality and sexuality in my clothing. It was really a great moment for me (because you know how interested I am in fashion) when I was in Spain, in Barcelona, one night a couple of summers ago, and the garbage collectors were out. They were all wearing bright orange uniforms and I was so thrilled. I remember growing up and never liking the garbage collectors because I saw them as somehow dirty people. One of the many articles I want to write about fashion has to do with how much in this culture we sort of make the job a person's identity. And I was so happy when I saw these men because they looked bright, they looked cheery, they looked like people you could look at. Usually their garb is sort of gray and drab and not something that is inviting, because it is not something that separates them from the task that they are doing and reminds us of their humanity and their dignity as people.

YZ: A lot of your analysis comes back to how capitalism underlies systems of oppression (correct me if I'm wrong), so is it a question of dismantling capitalism or is it a question of dismantling each of the systems of oppression...?
GW: Well, yeah, I was going to disagree with you. I think that a lot of my analysis comes back to an insistence upon interlocking systems of domination, something that I occasionally refer to as a "politic of domination." I think that capitalism is simply one manifestation of that politic of domination. I think that any form of socialism that places material values over human values can be equally integrated into a system of domination, so that I don't think that capitalism is the sole evil, let's eliminate it...but certainly I think that it is a central part of this system of domination that has to be dismantled.

YZ: So, when you are talking about a "politic of domination," that refers to all these interlocking systems of oppression—
GW: And it also refers to the ideological ground that they share, which is a belief in domination, and a belief in notions of superior and inferior, which are components of all of those systems. For me it's like a house, they share the foundation, but the foundation is the ideological beliefs around which notions of domination are constructed. One of them, which

I talk a lot about, certainly, in class, is Western metaphysical dualism. The whole notion of good, bad, evil, the triumph of good over evil and all of those kinds of notions.

YZ: What about the question that was asked at the end of your Law School talk, by Matt [Hamabata—Professor of Sociology]: why should men want to change, I mean what have they got invested in it?

GW: You know, the thing that really got me about that question, I thought about it for days, is that so many people expressed this real hard-core sense that men are never going to change. And I thought, can you imagine the despair of black people under slavery had we felt that there was nothing about that system that was going to change, that there was nothing about white people as a group, or as individuals, that would change? And it seems to me that, one of my favorite, favorite statements that I say a lot, which I didn't say that night because I was too tired, is the whole notion that "what we can't imagine, can't come to be." I feel like we've got to believe that men can change, and I believe profoundly that we have individual incidents of men changing. We can't discredit that reality by insisting there is nothing at stake for these people, that there is no hope that they will change. I mean, in a sense, it was very ironic that Matthew Hamabata would be asking this question. The very fact that a man such as he could be born into this world in an environment that was conducive to his identifying with women and with the struggle of women for liberation, to me, is a signifier of the possibility for change.

YZ: Well, then Matt continued his question, after you made the comparison of white people having changed, and he said, "well, I don't see white people giving up the reigns of power, really..." There may be huge changes, but still the white-supremacist, capitalist patriarchy remains intact.

GW: This is true. But I don't think that means that we're going to stop resisting that system, or that we're going to give up hope that it won't alter itself, or that it won't *be* altered, let us say, because it's not going to alter itself. And I don't think that one has to also see change as necessarily those in privilege giving up privilege. It may be those in privilege having that privilege taken away from them by the masses of people who don't share. And certainly, in revolutionary struggles all around the planet, we see this happening. We see a commitment on the part of oppressed peoples, certainly in places like Nicaragua and El Salvador, to struggle, and to make life very different and very difficult for those in privilege who oppress. But the talk was saying that there are men who are in pain, and it seems to me that feminist change could be a way out of that pain. Now, whether or not men will take that way out, I think that I would tend to feel very negatively about that. But I still think that we have to insist upon this as a space and a place for change.

25

black women and feminism

Toward the end of 1987 I spoke at Tufts University at an annual dinner for black women. My topic was "Black Women in Predominantly White Institutions." I was excited by the idea of talking with so many young black women but surprised when these women suggested that sexism was not a political issue of concern to black women, that the serious issue was racism. I've heard this response many times, yet somehow I did not expect that I would need to prove over and over that sexism ensures that many black females will be exploited and victimized. Confronted by these young black women to whom sexism was not important, I felt that feminism had failed to develop a politics that addresses black women. Particularly, I felt that black women active in black liberation struggles in the 1960s and early 1970s, who had spoken and written on sexism (remember the anthology *The Black Woman*, edited by Toni Cade Bambara?) had let our younger sisters down by not making more of a sustained political effort so that black women (and black people) would have greater understanding of the impact of sexist oppression on our lives.

When I began to share my own experiences of racism and sexism, pointing to incidents (particularly in relationships with black men), a veil was lifted. Suddenly the group acknowledged what had been previously denied—the ways sexism wounds us as black women. I had talked earlier about the way many black women students in predominantly white institutions keep silent in classes, stating emphatically that our progress in such places requires us to have a voice, to not remain silent. In the ensuing discussion, women commented on black fathers who had told their daughters "nobody wants a loud-talking black woman." The group expressed ambivalent feelings about speaking, particularly on political issues in classroom settings where they were often attacked or unsupported by other black women students.

Their earlier reluctance to acknowledge sexism reminded me of previous arguments with other groups of women about both the book and the film *The Color Purple*. Our discussions focused almost solely on whether portraying brutal sexist domination of a black female by a black male had any basis in reality. I was struck by the extent to which folks will go to argue that sexism in black communities has not promoted the abuse and subjugation of black women by black men. This fierce denial has its roots in the history of black people's response to racism and white supremacy. Traditionally it has been important for black people to assert that slavery, apartheid, and continued discrimination have not undermined the humanity of black people, that not only has the race been preserved but that the survival of black families and communities are the living testimony of our victory. To acknowledge then that our families and communities have been undermined by sexism would not only require an acknowledgement that racism is not the only form of domination and oppression that affects us as a people; it would mean critically challenging the assumption that our survival as a people depends on creating a cultural climate in which black men can achieve manhood within paradigms constructed by white patriarchy.

Often the history of our struggle as black people is made synonymous with the efforts of black males to have patriarchal power and privilege. As one black woman college student put it, "In order to redeem the race we have to redeem black manhood." If such redemption means creating a society in which black men assume the stereotypical male role of provider and head of household, then sexism is seen not as destructive but as essential to the promotion and maintenance of the black family. Tragically, it has been our acceptance of this model that has prevented us from acknowledging that black male sexist domination has *not* enhanced or enriched black family life. The seemingly positive aspects of the patriarchy (caretaker and provider) have been the most difficult for masses of black men to realize, and the negative aspects (maintaining control through psychological or physical violence) are practiced daily. Until black people redefine in a nonsexist revolutionary way the terms of our liberation, black women and men will always be confronted with the issue of whether supporting feminist efforts to end sexism is inimical to our interests as a people.

In her insightful essay, "Considering Feminism as a Model for Social Change," Sheila Radford-Hill makes the useful critique that black women producing feminist theory, myself included, focus more on the racism of white women within feminist movement, and on the importance of racial difference, than on the ways feminist struggle could strengthen and help black communities. In part, the direction of our work was shaped by the nature of our experience. Not only were there very few black women writing feminist theory, but most of us were not living in or working with black communities. The aim of *Ain't I A Woman* was not to focus on the racism of white women. Its primary purpose was to establish that sexism greatly determines the social status and experience of black women. I did not try to examine the ways that struggling to end sexism would benefit black people, but this is my current concern.

Many black women insist that they do not join the feminist movement because they cannot bond with white women who are racist. If one argues that there really are some white women who are resisting and challenging racism, who are genuinely committed to ending white supremacy, one is accused of being naive, of not acknowledging history. Most black women, rich and poor, have contact with white women, usually in work settings. In such settings black women cooperate with white women despite racism. Yet black women are reluctant to express solidarity with white feminists. Black women's consciousness is shaped by internalized racism and by reactionary white women's concerns as they are expressed in popular culture, such as daytime soap operas or in the world of white fashion and cosmetic products, which masses of black women consume without rejecting this racist propaganda and devaluing of black women.

Emulating white women or bonding with them in these "apolitical" areas is not consistently questioned or challenged. Yet I do not know a single black woman advocate of feminist politics who is not bombarded by ongoing interrogations by other black people about linking with racist white women (as though we lack the political acumen to determine whether white women are racists, or when it is in our interest to act in solidarity with them).

At times, the insistence that feminism is really "a white female thing that has nothing to do with black women" masks black female rage towards white women, a rage rooted in the historical servant-served relationship where white women have used power to dominate, exploit, and oppress. Many black women share this animosity, and it is evoked again and again when white women attempt to assert control over us. This resistance to white female domination must be separated from a black female refusal to bond with white women engaged in feminist struggle. This refusal is often rooted as well in traditional sexist models: women learn to see one another as enemies, as threats, as competitors. Viewing white women as competitors for jobs, for companions, for valuation in a culture that only values select groups of women, often serves as a barrier to bonding, even in settings where radical white women are not acting in a dominating manner. In some settings it has become a way of one-upping white women for black women to trivialize feminism.

Black women must separate feminism as a political agenda from white women or we will never be able to focus on the issue of sexism as it affects black communities. Even though there are a few black women (I am one) who assert that we empower ourselves by using the term feminism, by addressing our concerns as black women as well as our concern with the welfare of the human community globally, we have had little impact. Small groups of black feminist theorists and activists who use the term "black feminism" (the Combahee River Collective is one example) have not had much success in organizing large groups of black women, or stimulating widespread interest in feminist movement. Their statement of purpose and plans for action focus exclusively on black women acknowledging the need for forms of separatism. Here the argument that black women do not collectively advocate feminism because of an unwillingness to bond with racist white women appears most problematic. Key concerns that serve as barriers to black women advocating feminist politics are heterosexism, the fear that one will be seen as betraying black men or promoting hatred of men and as a consequence becoming less desirable to male companions; homophobia (often I am told by black people that all feminists are lesbians); and deeply ingrained misogynist attitudes toward one another, perpetuating sexist thinking and sexist competition.

Recently I spoke with a number of black women about why they are not more involved in feminist thinking and feminist movement. Many of them talked about harsh treatment by other black women, about being socially ostracized or talked about in negative and contemptuous ways at all-female gatherings or at conferences on gender issues. A few people committed to feminist politics described times when they found support from white women and resistance from black women peers. A black woman scheduled on a panel arrived late and couldn't find a seat in the room. When she entered and had been standing for a while, I greeted her warmly from the podium and encouraged her to join me as there were seats in front. Not only did she choose to stand, during the break she said to me, "How dare you embarrass me by asking me to come up front." Her tone was quite hostile. I was disturbed that she saw this gesture as an attempt to embarrass her rather than as a gesture of recognition. This is not an isolated case. There are many occasions when we witness the failure of black women to trust one another, when we approach one another with suspicion.

Years ago I attended a small conference with about 20 black women. We were to organize a national conference on black feminism. We came from various positions, politics, and sexual preferences. A well-known black woman scholar at a prestigious institution, whose feminist thinking was not deemed appropriately advanced, was treated with contempt and hostility. It was a disturbing time. A number of the black women present had white women companions and lovers. Yet concerning the issue of whether white women should be allowed to attend the conference, they were adamant that it should be for black women only, that white women all too often try to control us. There was no space for constructive critical dialogue. How could they trust white women lovers to unlearn racism, to not be dominating, and yet in this setting act as though all white women were our enemies? The conference never happened. At least one black woman went away from this experience determined never to participate in an activity organized around black feminists or any other feminists. As a group we failed to create an atmosphere of solidarity. The only bonds established were along very traditional lines among the folks who were famous, who talked the loudest and the most, who were more politically correct. And there was no attempt to enable black women with different perspectives to come together.

It is our collective responsibility as individual black women committed to feminist movement to work at making space where black women who are just beginning to explore feminist issues can do so without fear of hostile treatment, quick judgments, dismissals, etc.

I find more black women than ever before are appearing on panels that focus on gender. Yet I have observed, and other black women thinkers have shared as well, that often these women see gender as a subject for discourse or for increased professional visibility, not for political action. Often professional black women with academic degrees are quite conservative politically. Their perspectives differ greatly from our foremothers who were politically astute, assertive, and radical in their work for social change.

Feminist praxis is greatly shaped by academic women and men. Since there are not many academic black women committed to radical politics, especially with a gender focus, there is no collective base in the academy for forging a feminist politics that addresses masses of black women. There is much more work by black women on gender and sexism emerging from scholars who do literary criticism and from creative fiction and drama writers than from women in history, sociology, and political science. While it does not negate commitment to radical politics, in literature it is much easier to separate academic work and political concerns. Concurrently, if black women academics are not committed to feminist ethics, to feminist consciousness-raising, they end up organizing conferences in which social interactions mirror sexist norms, including ways black women regard one another. For the uninitiated coming to see and learn what feminism centered on black women might be like, this can be quite disillusioning.

Often in these settings the word "feminism" is evoked in negative terms, even though sexism and gender issues are discussed. I hear black women academics laying claim to the term "womanist" while rejecting "feminist." I do not think Alice Walker intended this term to deflect from feminist commitment, yet this is often how it is evoked. Walker defines womanist as black feminist or feminist of color. When I hear black women using the term womanist, it is in opposition to the term feminist; it is viewed as constituting something separate from feminist politics shaped by white women. For me, the term womanist is not sufficiently linked to a tradition of radical political commitment to struggle and change. What would a womanist politic look like? If it is a term for black feminist, then why do those who embrace it reject the other?

Radford-Hill makes the point:

> Not all black feminists practice or believe in black feminism. Many see black feminism as a vulgar detraction from the goal of female solidarity. Others of us, myself included, see black feminism as a necessary step toward ending racism and sexism, given the nature of gender oppression and the magnitude of society's resistance to racial justice.

I believe that women should think less in terms of feminism as an identity and more in terms of "advocating feminism"; to move from emphasis on personal lifestyle issues toward creating political paradigms and radical models of social change that emphasize collective as well as individual change. For this reason I do not call myself a black feminist. Black women must continue to insist on our right to participate in shaping feminist theory and practice that addresses our racial concerns as well as our feminist issues. Current feminist scholarship can be useful to black women in formulating critical analyses of gender issues about black people, particularly feminist work on parenting. (When I first read Dorothy Dinnerstein, it was interesting to think about her work in terms of black mother-son relationships.)

Black women need to construct a model of feminist theorizing and scholarship that is inclusive, that widens our options, that enhances our understanding of black experience and gender. Significantly, the most basic task confronting black feminists (irrespective of the terms we use to identify ourselves) is to educate one another and black people about sexism, about the ways resisting sexism can empower black women, a process which makes sharing feminist vision more difficult. Radford-Hill identifies "the crisis of black womanhood" as a serious problem that must be considered politically, asserting that "the extent to which black feminists can articulate and solve the crisis of black womanhood is the extent to which black women will undergo feminist transformation."

Black women must identify ways feminist thought and practice can aid in our process of self-recovery and share that knowledge with our sisters. This is the base on which to build political solidarity. When that grounding exists, black women will be fully engaged in feminist movement that transforms self, community, and society.

bibliography

anonymous, *Women and the New World*, 1976.

Anzaldúa, Gloria, *Borderlands: La Frontera*, San Francisco: Spinsters Ink, 1987.

Aptheker, Bettina, *Woman's Legacy: Essays on Race, Sex, and Class*, Amherst, MA: University of Massachusetts Press, 1982.

Argueta, Manlio, *One Day of Life*, New York: Vintage Books, 1983.

Bambara, Toni Cade, ed., *The Black Woman*, New York: New American Library, 1970.

Bambara, Toni Cade, *The Salteaters*, New York: Random House, 1980.

Bell, Derrick, *And We Are Not Saved: The Elusive Quest for Racial Justice*, New York: Basic Books, 1987.

Breitman, George, *The Last Year of Malcolm X—The Evolution of a Revolutionary*, New York: Pathfinder Press, 1970.

Brooks, Gwendolyn, *Maud Martha*, New York: AMS Press, 1974.

Building Feminist Theory: Essays from Quest, New York: Longman, 1981.

Bunch, Charlotte, *Passionate Politics*, New York: St. Martin's Press, 1987.

Bunch, Charlotte and Myron, Nancy, *Class and Feminism*, Baltimore: Diana Press, 1974.

Cagan, Leslie, "Talking Disarmament," in *South End Press News, Vol. 2, No. 2 (Spring/Summer 1983), pp. 1-7*.

Eisenstein, Zillah, *The Radical Future of Liberal Feminism*, New York: Longman, 1981.

Freire, Paulo, *Pedagogy of the Oppressed,* New York: Herder and Herden, 1970.

Frye, Marilyn, *The Politics of Reality: Essays in Feminist Theory,* Trumansburg, NY: Crossing Press, 1983.

Haug, Frigga, *Female Sexualization: A Collective Work of Memory,* London: Verso, 1987.

Hemingway, *The Sun Also Rises,* New York: Scribner, 1970.

Heresies #15: Racism is the Issue, 1982.

Hodge, John, ed., *Cultural Bases of Racism and Group Oppression,* Berkeley: Two Readers Press, 1975.

Irigaray, Luce, *Speculum of the Other Women,* Ithaca, NY: Cornell University Press, 1985.

Johnson, James Weldon, *The Book of American Negro Poetry,* New York: Harcourt, Brace and Co., 1958.

Koen, Susan; Swain, Nina; and Friends, *Ain't Nowhere We Can Run: A Handbook For Women on the Nuclear Mentality,* Norwich, VT: WAND, 1980.

Kristeva, Julia, *Desire in Language,* New York: Columbia University Press, 1980.

Lorde, Audre, *Sister Outsider,* Trumansburg, NY: Crossing Press, 1984.

Mellen, Joan, *Women and Their Sexuality in the New Film,* London: David-Poynter, 1974.

Morrison, Toni, *The Bluest Eye,* New York: Holt, Rinehart and Winston, 1970.

Morrison, Toni, *Sula,* New York: Knopf, 1973.

Naylor, Gloria, *The Women of Brewster Place,* New York: Penguin Books, 1982.

Partnoy, Alicia, *The Little School: Tales of Disappearance and Survival in Argentina,* Pittsburgh: Cleis Press, 1986.

Petry, Ann, *The Street,* New York: Pyramid Books, 1946.

Rodriguez, Richard, *Hunger of Memory,* Boston: David Godine, 1982.

Ruddick, Sara, *Working It Out,* New York: Pantheon, 1977.

Russ, Joanna, *How to Suppress Women's Writing,* Austin, TX: University of Texas Press, 1983.

Smith, Barbara, ed., *Home Girls,* New York: Kitchen Table/Women of Color Press, 1983.

Stack, Carol, *All Our Kin,* New York: Harper & Row, 1974.

Van Sertima, Ivan, *They Came Before Columbus,* New York: Random House, 1976.

Walker, Alice, *The Color Purple,* New York: Washington Square Press, 1982.

Walker, Lenore, *The Battered Woman,* New York: Harper & Row, 1979.

X, Malcolm, *The Autobiography of Malcolm X,* New York: Grove, 1964.